Monthly Mini-Lessons:
Forty Projects for Independent Study, Grades 2 and 3

by

Mary A. Lombardo

LINWORTH LEARNING

Activities & Resources From the Minds of Teachers

Library of Congress Cataloging-in-Publication Data

Lombardo, Mary A.
  Monthly mini-lessons : forty projects for independent study, grades 2 and
3 / by Mary A. Lombardo.
      p. cm.
  Includes bibliographical references and index.
  ISBN 1-58683-196-8 (pbk. : alk. paper)
  1. Independent study. 2. Project method in teaching. I. Title.
LB1601.3.L662 2005
372.1139'4--dc22
                          2005013160

Published by Linworth Publishing, Inc.
480 East Wilson Bridge Road, Suite L
Worthington, Ohio 43085

1-58683-196-8

5 4 3 2 1

Table of Contents

Table of Contents | CONTINUED

Table of Contents | CONTINUED

Table of Contents | CONTINUED

Table of Contents | CONTINUED

About the Author

Mary Lombardo is a retired teacher who has taught all grade levels from one through six as well as Title 1 reading to at-risk students. For several years she worked in an alternative public school program for home-schooled students, providing curriculum and teaching assistance to parents and half-day instruction to students. She also served as a teacher trainer for the Albuquerque Public Schools.

Overview

This book is intended to foster independent study, research, writing, and oral presentation skills for students in grades two and three. The lessons, which integrate several content areas, can be used for enrichment or extension activities in the classroom or for homework assignment. After the included short, teacher - led introduction to the subject matter, students will be able to complete the study sheets that accompany each lesson alone or with a cooperative group. The 40 lessons, four for each of 10 months, September through June, are connected to a famous person or event associated with that month. An index indicates the content areas and skills emphasized in each lesson.

Teacher Introduction

All classroom and homework assignments need to be meaningful activities that help students apply skills learned, as well as provide them with an opportunity to work independently or as a contributing part of a group. As the students work through the chapters in this book, they will be applying skills learned in many curricular areas, as well as using creativity and critical thinking to complete the assignments.

Organization of the Book

There are 40 lessons, four for each month of the school year. All lessons are connected to some event or person associated with the month where it is presented, and each contains background information for the teacher, introductory classroom activities, and a student handout for independent work. The lessons are organized chronologically so that they can be presented in the month that corresponds with the person or event under study, and skills/content areas are listed in each lesson in their order of occurrence. Teachers wishing students to practice a skill that corresponds with other classroom lessons can use the index to locate specific skills and content areas.

Objectives

1. To promote independent study and group work.

2. To promote research skills, critical thinking, and creativity.

3. To promote meaningful activities that allow students to apply skills and content standards they have learned.

4. To provide students the opportunity to use different forms of writing, both fiction and nonfiction.

5. To provide the opportunity to make oral presentations before an audience.

6. To introduce students to famous historical figures and events.

7. To support art, health, interesting geographical and scientific phenomena, and make mathematical applications.

How to Use this Book

You can use this book in many different ways. The lessons can be assigned each week of the school year as contracts with the students. For example, on Monday, review the background material for the lesson with the students, engage in some or all of the accompanying activities, and distribute the student handout, due on Friday. The handout can be assigned to be done in a specified classroom time independently, with a partner or cooperative group, or as work to be done at home.

The assignments are designed to be easily corrected through student exchange and/or sharing in the classroom. The instructions tell students to put writing exercises on separate papers so you can review them at another time. The teacher notes include advice for emphasizing and correcting only one function in each writing exercise or oral presentation. For instance, after advising the students to focus on mechanics in a writing assignment, you would score only that skill.

The lessons do not have to be used chronologically. If you decide students need extra practice with specific skills or in specific content areas, use the index to locate lessons that will meet that need. In fact, because students differ in their instructional needs, it might be helpful to assign lessons to individual students as they exhibit a need that is emphasized in the lesson.

Here's another way to use the lessons in this book. Each month, choose four students or pairs of students and assign them a different lesson for that month. As the students complete the lesson they report on it to the class, providing an opportunity to give an oral report as they teach their fellow students what they have learned.

Correlation with NCTE Standards*

The National Council of Teachers of English has developed 12 standards citing how students should be helped to develop appropriate language skills. The exercises in *Monthly Mini - Lessons* provide students the opportunity to use language in a variety of ways and help teachers incorporate NCTE Standards into their curricula.

* A complete list of standards can be found at http://www.ncte.org.
In addition, because several content areas are integrated into the lessons, you may want to list content standards for those areas as well when planning instruction.

Assessment

Each lesson includes suggestions for efficient assessment of student work. Many of the assignments can be evaluated as a whole class activity with the teacher looking over students' work as they share it with the class. This is the time you can make note of complete or incomplete assignments as well as areas of concern such as inability to use reference materials, poor understanding of math functions, etc.

The only formal assessment suggested is for written compositions and oral presentations. These can be scored on a variety of skills, but each lesson suggests assessing only one skill for each piece of writing or presentation. This tactic will not only save time, but also will allow students to concentrate on one area for each written and oral assignment.

Following are rubrics to be used in grading written and oral work and also a list of questions to help you assess work quality, skill application, and content knowledge.

Peer Assessment

Another tactic that will save time and also be of great value for the students is to teach them how to assess each other's work. Even very young students can learn to evaluate another's writing or speaking and, when they do, they become more attuned to what they should be doing when they write or give a presentation themselves.

Post the rubrics in the classroom and explain how they can be used in scoring. Give examples of work that might be scored 1, 2, or 3. Practice on a few written compositions and compare why the students have selected the score they did. Do the same for oral presentations.

For written work, review the skill being assessed, making sure the students understand how the rubric is used, have students trade papers, and give adequate classroom time for scoring. Ask students to write the score, one sentence explaining why they chose that score, and their own name at the top of the paper. Collect the papers.

To facilitate assessing oral reports, divide the class into groups of four or five students each. Have each student list on a piece of paper the names of everyone in their group including themselves. Review the rubrics for the particular area being assessed and have the students give their presentation to their small group. Each student selects a score and in one sentence explains why they selected that score. The presenter self-scores. Collect the scoring sheets.

Teaching students to assess their own work and that of others will take a little more time initially, but it will prove to be an efficient way to score compositions and presentations and will help improve students' writing and speaking capabilities.

Work Ethic, Skills, and Content Assessment

In addition to using the rubrics listed below for scoring written and oral work, you will want to assess how the students are applying skills and information presented in each lesson as well as the quality of their work. Inform the students that you will be assessing them in these areas along with the written and oral assignments. As the class shares their completed assignments, record your observations in a grade book. You might want to transfer your observations to a wall chart so each student can see what skills or work habits they excel at or need to improve. Here is a list of possible questions you may want to use as an aid.

Is the student's work complete?

Is the work neatly done?

Is the work organized?

Does the student seem to have an understanding of the subject matter? (geographic concepts, sense of history, time placement of historical events, scientific phenomena?)

Has the student applied learned skills in using reference books, writing letters, carrying out math functions, etc?

Rubrics: Written Assignments

Creativity:
1 - Things you've heard before
2 - Some new ideas
3 - A lot of new ideas

Organization:
1 – Things happen out of order
2 – Parts of it are in order
3 – Most everything seems in the right order

Mechanics:
1 - A lot of mistakes
2 - At least half has no mistakes
3 - Very few or no mistakes

Neatness:
1 – Messy and hard to read
2 - Some messy parts, but okay to read
3 - Neat and easy to read

Content:
1 – Does not seem to understand the subject
2 – Seems to know something about the subject
3 - Understands a lot about the subject

Rubrics: Oral Presentations

Body Language:
1 - No movement or gestures
2 - Makes some gestures
3 - Movements help keep interest

Pacing:
1 - Too fast or too slow most of the time
2 - Too fast or too slow some of the time
3 - Does not speak too fast or too slow

Eye Contact:
1 - Never looks up at audience
2 - Looks up at audience at least half of the time
3 - Looks at the audience a lot

Organization:
1 – Order doesn't make sense
2 – Parts of the talk are in the right order
3 – Everything is in the right order

Chapter 1 | September

S E P T	E M	B E R				
				1	2	3
4	5	6	7	8	9	10
11	12	13	14	15	16	17
18	19	20	21	22	23	24
25	26	27	28	29	30	

Assignment 1 | The Star Spangled Banner

Assignment 2 | Hurricane

Assignment 3 | When Autumn Comes

Assignment 4 | The Calendar

Assignment 1 | The Star-Spangled Banner

Skills: art: drawing; reference: dictionary; writing: essay; critical thinking

The Star-Spangled Banner Background for Teachers

- The year was 1812. Britain was at war with France and needed sailors to man its warships. So British ships began stopping American ships at sea, kidnapping American sailors, and forcing them to fight for Britain. President James Madison asked for a declaration of war against Great Britain in order to protect American ships at sea. He also wanted to keep Britain from allying with Native Americans because he wanted to annex Florida and Canada. The War of 1812 ended in a draw because Britain was too busy fighting France to wage another war, and the United States was not prepared for a fight.

- In 1814, Francis Scott Key, from a ship in Baltimore Harbor, witnessed the British attacking Fort McHenry. Seeing the American flag flying over the fort the next day at daybreak, he was inspired to write a poem entitled, *The Star-Spangled Banner*. He chose an old English tune to accompany the words he had written and that's how the Star-Spangled Banner came to be. In 1931, the song he wrote became the official national anthem for the United States of America.

The Star-Spangled Banner Activities

1. Discuss how the Star-Spangled Banner came to be written. Discuss how Francis Scott Key must have felt when he saw the flag still flying on the morning after the battle. Dissect the song, eliciting from the students what they think the words mean.

2. Play a recording of several patriotic songs. Discuss the lyrics and their meaning.

3. Explain that in a personal essay, people write their personal opinions and feelings and that everyone's feelings are valid. There is no right or wrong opinion!

✔ **Assessment:** Have students form small groups to share what they drew to decorate the anthem, the definitions, and their essays. Score the written composition on mechanics.

The Star Spangled Banner—Student Handout

Name _____ Date _____

1. The Star – Spangled Banner became our national anthem in 1931. If you cannot say the words by heart, now is the time to study and memorize them. Decorate around the copy of the song below. Draw and color pictures that give an idea of what was happening the night Francis Scott Key wrote it.

The Star-Spangled Banner

O, say can you see, by the dawn's early light
What so proudly we hailed, at the twilight's last gleaming.
Whose broad stripes and bright stars through the perilous fight
O'er the ramparts we watched were so gallantly streaming.
And the rockets red glare, the bombs bursting in air,
Gave proof through the night that our flag was still there.
Oh, say does that star – spangled banner yet wave,
O'er the land of the free and the home of the brave.

2. What do these words from the song mean?

Dawn _____

Twilight _____

Perilous _____

Ramparts _____

3. There are many songs written about the United States of America and its flag. All of the songs talk abut the freedom to be found in the United States. On another piece of paper, tell why you think the United States is called the "land of the free."

Assignment 2 | Hurricane

Skills: geography: hurricane locations; science: hurricane; critical thinking; writing: fiction

Hurricane Background for Teachers

- Hurricanes are storms that start over the ocean near the equator especially in the Caribbean Sea and the Gulf of Mexico. Basically they are high winds blowing in a circular direction around a low-pressure center called the "eye of the storm."

- The eye of the hurricane is about 15 miles wide. In this area, there are no clouds or wind.

- Hurricanes are rated from one to five, with one being the mildest storm. In a number one hurricane, winds may be around 75 miles an hour, whereas the winds in a number five hurricane can be as strong as 155 miles per hour. Number five hurricanes are very rare but have occurred.

- Hurricanes travel at varying speeds. Some travel as slowly as five miles per hour while others can travel as fast as 50 miles per hour.

- Since the origin of the National Hurricane Center in Florida which tracks all hurricanes from beginning to end, many lives have been saved because of accurate predictions of where hurricanes are headed. Unfortunately loss of property is still high.

Hurricane Activities

1. Share what students know about hurricanes.

2. Since this is hurricane season, find newspaper articles about current storms and discuss them. Trace their route on a map.

3. Stock the classroom library with books about hurricanes. Schedule classroom time so students can choose and read one or two.

> ✓ **Assessment:** List on the board all the countries, states, or islands the students have found that are in or near the Gulf of Mexico and the Caribbean Sea. Locate them on a map. Explain that these places are usually where hurricanes cause the most damage. Compare drawings of a hurricane. Score the written assignment for creativity.

Hurricane Student Handout

Name _____ Date _____

1. A hurricane is a storm that starts over the ocean near the equator especially in the Caribbean Sea and the Gulf of Mexico. Find these two bodies of water on a map. Make a list of at least 10 countries and islands that are in or near them.

   1. _____   6. _____
   2. _____   7. _____
   3. _____   8. _____
   4. _____   9. _____
   5. _____   10. _____

2. Hurricanes are made of high winds blowing in a circle around a center called the "eye of the storm." The eye of the hurricane is about 15 miles wide. There are no clouds or wind in the "eye." In the space below, draw a picture of what you think a hurricane looks like. Show with arrows the direction the circle of wind is going and label the "eye" of the storm.

3. Hurricanes can destroy many things when they cross over land. The winds can blow roofs off buildings and trees out of the ground, and the rain causes floods that carry everything in their path away. Imagine a family in a place where a hurricane was going to pass. They have no time to go somewhere else to wait until the storm passes. What would they do to stay safe? How do they feel? Are they scared? Excited? On a separate piece of paper, write a story about how they are feeling as the hurricane gets near and what they do to keep the family together and safe.

Assignment 3 | When Autumn Comes

Skills: science: earth's movements, seasons, and trees; writing: essay

When Autumn Comes Background for Teachers

- Autumn begins on September 21 or 22. This date is also called the Autumnal Equinox. Equinox means equal night and it is a time when there are equal amounts of day and night: 12 hours of each. At the time of the equinox the sun crosses directly over the earth's equator at noon. After this, in the northern hemisphere, nights begin to get longer until winter begins in the middle of December, at the winter Solstice, when they begin to get shorter again. In the southern hemisphere, the seasons are exactly opposite.

- The only other time the sun is directly over the equator at noon is at the start of Spring, or at the Vernal equinox, which occurs around March 20 or 21.

- Normally the earth's axis is tilted either toward or away from the sun; at the beginning of Autumn and the beginning of Spring, the earth's axis is at a right angle to the sun.

- Autumn is when the leaves of deciduous trees turn brilliant colors and fall to the ground. Non-deciduous or evergreen trees keep their color all year long.

When Autumn Comes Activities

1. Using a globe and a light source, demonstrate the earth's tilt in relation to the sun. Start at the autumnal equinox with the earth's axis at a right angle to the sun. Then slowly begin to tilt it away from the sun to show that winter is coming to the northern hemisphere with shorter days and longer nights and summer to the summer hemisphere with longer days and shorter nights.

2. Demonstrate how to draw the earth showing the equator and the poles and how the earth looks tilted toward the sun and away from it.

3. Discuss the characteristics of deciduous and non – deciduous or evergreen trees.

 Assessment: Share and discuss drawings. Post the examples of foliage on a bulletin board. Pair students to share essays and score for organization.

When Autumn Comes Handout

Name _____ Date _____

1. The sun is always in the same place in the sky. The earth tilts toward or away from the sun causing the seasons. When Autumn comes, the earth begins to tilt away from the sun. The days get shorter and the nights get longer. Draw a picture here of the sun and the earth tilting away from it. Label the sun and Earth.

AUTUMN

When Summer comes, the earth tilts toward the sun. The days get longer and the nights shorter. Draw a picture here of the sun and the earth tilting toward the sun. Label the sun and Earth.

SUMMER

2. In the autumn of the year, leaves on deciduous trees change color and fall to the ground. Evergreen trees stay green all year long. On the back of this paper, tape some examples of leaves from deciduous trees and foliage from evergreen trees and label them.

3. On a separate piece of paper, write at least two paragraphs showing how your life is different in the summer and the autumn.

Assignment 4 | The Calendar

Skills: math: addition; writing: essay; critical thinking

 ## The Calendar Background for Teachers

■ The first calendar was a lunar calendar designed by the Babylonians. They based it on the phases of the moon and counted 12 lunar months to a year with each month containing 30 days. Every four years, they added a thirteenth month so the seasons would agree with the calendar.

■ The Greeks and Egyptians adopted this calendar, but the Egyptians later switched to a calendar that matched the arrival of the seasons more closely. Their calendar was based on the solar year of 365 days. There were 12 months of 30 days each with five extra days at the end of each year. In 238 BC, King Ptolemy III ordered that an extra day be added every fourth year.

■ In 45 BC, Julius Caesar adopted the Julian calendar of 365 days with one extra day added every four years. He established the order of the months, naming July after himself. August is named after Augustus Caesar. In 1582, Pope Gregory authorized the use of the Gregorian calendar which dropped 10 days from the Julian Calendar, again to coordinate with the seasons. This calendar is used in most of the world today. On September 14, 1752, Great Britain and its colonies adopted the Gregorian calendar.

The Calendar Activities

1. Show a calendar. Make sure the students know the names and order of the months.

2. Tell the students some of the history of the calendar so they will realize it was developed over many, many years.

3. Discuss the idea of a solar calendar that is based on the time it takes the earth to travel around the sun.

4. Teach or review adding columns of numbers and carrying.

Assessment: On a large piece of chart paper, write the names of the months and, beneath their names, list the events the students have named. Go over math totals together. Group the students to share essays and score the written assignment or organization.

The Calendar Student Handout

Name _____ Date _____

1. There are twelve months in the year. List the months below in the correct order and next to each name write something that happens in that month. It could be a holiday like New Year's Day, or a birthday of someone you know, or the start of a new season, or the month your grandma comes to visit!

    1. _____
    2. _____
    3. _____
    4. _____
    5. _____
    6. _____
    7. _____
    8. _____
    9. _____
    10. _____
    11. _____
    12. _____

2. Our calendar is based on how long it takes for the earth to travel around the sun.

    a) Add the number of days in
       September
       April
       June
       November.   +_____
       Total

    b) Add the number of days in
       January
       March
       May
       July   +_____
       Total

    c) Add the number of days in
       August
       October
       December
       February   +_____
       Total

    d) Now add all your totals.
       total from a:
       total from b:
       total from c: +_____
       days in a year

    How long does it take the earth to travel around the sun? _____

3. What month of the year is your favorite? On a separate piece of paper, write at least two paragraphs telling all the reasons why that month is your favorite one. Think about these questions: what are the special things you do, what's the weather like, what do you wear, do you take trips?

Chapter 2 | October

O C T O B E R						
						1
2	3	4	5	6	7	8
9	10	11	12	13	14	15
16	17	18	19	20	21	22
23/30	24/31	25	26	27	28	29

Assignment 5 | Webster's Dictionary

Skills: reference: dictionary; graphic organizer: chart; writing: essay

Webster's Dictionary Background for Teachers

- Noah Webster was born on October 16, 1758. He was a lexicographer, a person who writes or compiles a dictionary. Webster was a man of many talents. He studied law, graduated from Yale, taught school, fought in the American Revolution, and was a prolific writer. He wrote on many subjects: medicine, politics, economics and physical science. He also started two newspapers.

- A spelling book he wrote, the *Elementary Spelling Book*, is still in print in a revised form. His first dictionary, a very short one, was completed in 1806. In 1828, when he was 70 years old, he completed the *American Dictionary of the English Language*. His dictionary has been edited many times since that date and is still in use today.

- Noah Webster died in 1843, but his work lives on today in many of the dictionaries we use.

Webster's Dictionary Activities

1. Review how to use a dictionary, including use of guide words, and identification of parts of speech.

2. Play a game. Write a word on the board and ask the students to guess what it means. Then have them look it up in the dictionary to see if anyone guessed correctly.

3. Talk about what a lexicographer does and about Noah Webster in particular. Is this a field any student would want to choose? Why or why not?

 Assessment: Share definitions and chart. Play the dictionary game in class with some of the words the students used. Group the class to share their essays and score the essay on organization.

Webster's Dictionary Student Handout

Name _____ Date _____

1. Noah Webster was a lexicographer. Look up lexicographer in the dictionary and write what it means here.

   A lexicographer is _____

   _____

   _____

2. The dictionary that Noah Webster wrote is still used today. Look at dictionaries at home, at school, and at the library. How many did you find that have Webster's name in the title?

   _____

3. Here is a game you can play with your friends. Find five funny sounding words in a dictionary. On the back of this paper, write their meanings down. Ask your friends to guess what the words mean. Then tell the real meanings.

   For example, what would you say *cress* means? Put your guess here.

   _____

   Then look it up in the dictionary and write its real meaning here.

   _____

4. Guide words are the first word and last word on each dictionary page. They make it easier for you to find a word you are looking for. Look up 10 words in your dictionary. Then, on a separate piece of paper, make a chart that lists the words and gives the guide words for the dictionary page where you found them.

5. Dictionaries change all the time. Lexicographers find new words that people are using and put them in the dictionary. What do you think would be more interesting to do: write a make believe story or discover new words to include in a dictionary? Why? On another piece of paper, write at least two paragraphs telling why you think one job would be more interesting than the other.

Assignment 6 | Fire Prevention Week

Skill: critical thinking; art: poster; writing: slogans, fiction

Fire Prevention Week Background for Teachers

- The story goes that on October 8, 1871 at nine o'clock in the evening, Mrs. O'Leary's cow kicked over a lantern and started the Great Chicago fire. However the fire started, almost 100,000 people lost their homes and the damages cost around $200,000,000. Fire Prevention Week is held near the date of this terrible fire.

- The Smokey Bear campaign was created in 1944 as a public service to prevent fires, and the message of the campaign remained the same until 2001 when it was expanded to address the growing number of wildfires in our public lands. Actually Smokey Bear was a real black bear cub who had climbed a tall tree to escape a raging wildfire in New Mexico. That saved his life but, when rescuers found him, his paws and hind legs were badly burned. He was flown to a veterinarian in Santa Fe and later placed at the National Zoo in Washington DC.

- Before there were modern fire trucks with hoses, fires were put out by men in "bucket brigades." People stood in a line and passed buckets of water along to empty on the fire. Today we have much more efficient fire trucks and equipment, and modern firemen focus not only on putting out fires, but also on teaching how to prevent fires.

Fire Prevention Week Activities

1. Form a "bucket brigade" to illustrate how long it took to put out fires before hoses were used. Line the students up with one end of the line at the water source and the other end at an empty coffee can. Students pass along cups of water until the can is filled.

2. Talk about causes of fires and how they can be prevented.

3. Distribute large pieces of construction paper for the poster.

 Assessment: Post posters. Discuss how forest fires start, ideas for fire prevention, and the hazards they may have found in their homes. Score written assignment on creativity.

Fire Prevention Week Student Handout

Name _____ Date _____

1. a) Smokey Bear was a real bear who was saved from a forest fire. How do you think the fire started that almost took Smokey's life?

   _____

   _____

   _____

   b) How are some other ways forest fires can start?

   _____

   _____

   _____

2. Smokey Bear reminds us to be careful when we are in the woods. Choose a different animal to teach people to be careful in the woods. Draw your animal on a large piece of paper. Under its picture, write one way to prevent forest fires.

3. Fires can start in other places besides forests. They can start in our homes or our neighborhoods. With an adult, look through your home to see if there are any places where fire might start. Check off the list below as you look, and add anything you wish.

   ☐ Wires with tears or cracks. _____

   ☐ Matches in a place where children can reach. _____

   ☐ Curtains near stoves. _____

   ☐ Ashtrays overflowing. _____

   ☐ Fireplace full of ashes. _____

   ☐ Smoke alarms not in working order. _____

   ☐ Furnace filters that need cleaning. _____

4. When forests and woods burn, the animals that live there often have no other place for their homes. On a separate piece of paper, write a story about some animals who have had to leave their home because of fire. Where do they go? How do they get there? Whom do they meet on the way? Who helps them?

Assignment 7 | A New World

Skills: reference: encyclopedia; geography; writing: biography and essay; health: self knowledge

A New World Background for Teachers

- Although there is evidence that others visited the Americas before Christopher Columbus, it is he who is credited with "discovering" the new world, perhaps because he established the first known European colony in the New World, La Isabela in the Dominican Republic. Whether we approve of Columbus' actions toward the natives he encountered or not, we have something to learn from his patience and persistence.

- Christopher Columbus had the idea that if he sailed to the west he would find a shorter route to the East where the exotic spices that Europeans loved so much originated. In 1484, he proposed his idea to the King of Portugal who rejected it.

- Columbus then moved to Spain and submitted his proposal to King Ferdinand and Queen Isabella in 1486. After four years, the commission they appointed to study the proposal recommended against funding it. Columbus did not give up. He reworked his proposal and submitted it again and this time it was approved. In 1492, eight years after his original proposal, Columbus sailed with his three ships, the Nina, the Pinta, and the Santa Maria, and the blessings of the King and Queen of Spain.

A New World Activities

1. Either read or tell the story of Columbus to the students.

2. Find the countries Portugal and Spain on a map and identify the ocean Columbus crossed to the new world.

3. On a map find the places where Columbus landed: the Bahamas, Cuba, Dominican Republic, Dominica, Guadeloupe, Antigua, and Puerto Rico.

4. Review what a biography is.

 Assessment: Make a chart listing the five explorers and Columbus. Fill in the chart with the information the students have found. Compare definitions and information on islands. Group students to share written compositions and score essay on creativity.

A New World Student Handout

Name _____ Date _____

1. Christopher Columbus is remembered for discovering America. In the past there have been many other explorers who were the first to see some part of America. Pick one of these men and tell when he lived, where he was from, and why he is remembered. Use the back of this paper for your work.

   Vasco De Gama   Ferdinand Magellan   Leif Ericson
   Ponce De Leon   Meriwether Lewis

2. Columbus visited many islands on his voyage to the New World. He visited the Bahamas, Cuba, the Dominican Republic, Haiti, Guadeloupe, Antigua, and Puerto Rico Look up *island* in the encyclopedia. Write what an island is.
   An island is _____

   _____

   Tell how an island is made.

   _____

   _____

   _____

   _____

   _____

   _____

   _____

3. Christopher Columbus had an idea that if he sailed west he would reach the Far East quicker than was then possible. The King of Portugal said no when he asked for ships. The King and Queen of Spain said no, too. He asked again and the King and Queen of Spain said yes and gave him three ships. Christopher Columbus was persistent and patient. He did not give up. He had confidence in himself and his ideas.

   Is it good to be like Columbus in those ways?

   On another piece of paper, write a few paragraphs telling whether you are like Columbus in those ways. Give examples that show how you are like or not like him.

Assignment 8 | Dinosaurs

Skills: geography; art: drawing; writing: book review

Di)nosaurs Background for Teachers

- On October 4, 1915, the Dinosaur National Monument was established on the Colorado and Utah border. The quarry at this monument in southeastern Utah is famous for fossilized remains of dinosaurs. In fact, more different kinds of dinosaur remains have been found here than at any other site in the world. Paleontologists have found many whole or almost whole dinosaur skeletons, many skulls in good condition, and many bones of young dinosaurs. Through the years, over 350 tons of bones have been removed from the quarry at the National Monument. Today paleontologists leave bones where they find them and visitors can view them in an exhibit that has over 1500 bones in their original place in the rock. At the visitors' center and museum, visitors can see a working paleontology lab and exhibits about the quarry and the dinosaurs that left their remains there.

- Dinosaur remains have been found in many parts of the United States. Most sites are in the western part of the country in Alaska, Arizona, New Mexico, Texas, Colorado, Utah, Wyoming, South Dakota, Montana, and Oklahoma. There are also some sites in eastern seaboard states in New Jersey, Maryland, Connecticut, and Massachusetts.

Dinosaurs Activities

1. On a map, locate Utah, site of the Dinosaur National Monument, and other states where dinosaur remains have been found.

2. Set up a dinosaur book corner, and give time for students to choose a book or two.

3. Ask students to brainstorm words that remind them of dinosaurs. Write the words randomly on a large piece of butcher block paper suitable for a mural, leaving room for pictures the students will draw. Distribute a piece of drawing paper.

 Assessment: Share information about states and meanings of dinosaur names. Paste drawings on mural, and display in the classroom. Score written assignment on mechanics.

Dinosaurs Student Handout

Name _____ Date _____

1. Dinosaur bones have been found all over the United States. Some places are in the eastern part of the country, but most are in the west in Alaska, Arizona, New Mexico, Texas, Colorado, Utah, Wyoming, South Dakota, Montana, and Oklahoma.

   The Dinosaur National Monument in southeastern Utah is famous for fossilized remains of dinosaurs. More different kinds of dinosaur remains have been found there than at any other place in the world. On a map, find Utah. List the six states that touch or border Utah and put a check next to the name of each one where dinosaur remains have been found.

   1. _____   4. _____

   2. _____   5. _____

   3. _____   6. _____

2. When the people studying dinosaurs began to name them, they picked words from the Greek or Latin languages. Here are the meanings of some of the words they picked.

   baro = heavy   dino = terrible   stego = plated
   cerato = horned   saur or saurus = lizard   bronto = thunder

   Look at the meanings to help you tell what the names of these dinosaurs mean.

   Dinosaur = _____

   Barosaurus = _____

   Ceratosaurus = _____

   Stegosaurus = _____

   Brontosaurus = _____

3. Choose a book about dinosaurs. Pick your favorite dinosaur and draw and color a picture of it on drawing paper. Write its name below it.

4. Write a book review of the book about dinosaurs. Give the title, the author's name, and tell what the book is about. Share some things you have learned. Then tell if you liked or did not like the book and why.

Chapter 3 | November

N	O	V	E	M	B	E	R
		1	2	3	4	5
6	7	8	9	10	11	12
13	14	15	16	17	18	19
20	21	22	23	24	25	26
27	28	29	30			

Assignment 9 | Mickey Mouse

Skills: critical thinking; art: flip book, drawing; writing; biography, description; oral presentation

Mickey Mouse Background for Teachers

- November 18, 1928, is the "birth date" of Mickey Mouse. His creator, Walt Disney, introduced him in a cartoon called *Plane Crazy*.

- Walt Disney was born in Chicago in 1901. He left school when he was 16, but later attended art school and, in 1923, began producing animated motion pictures with his brother Roy. Basically animation is created by recording people or things in a series of pictures that show slight movement from one picture to the next.

- Of all the characters Disney created, Mickey seems to be the most popular and enduring figure. Children enjoyed a television show, The Mickey Mouse Club, for many years. At Disneyland in California and Disney World in Florida, a bigger than life Mickey Mouse can be seen wandering about, posing with children of all sizes and ages.

- Walt Disney died in 1966 after winning 26 Academy Awards.

Mickey Mouse Activities

1. Discuss various cartoon characters that the children are familiar with.

2. Share stories of trips to Disneyland or Disney World and Mickey sightings.

3. Talk about how animation is developed by demonstrating how to make a flip book.

   Make a book by stapling 10 or 12 pieces of paper together (4"x 5"). On the front of each page draw the same person or object, with each picture showing a small bit of movement so that when the pictures are flipped through, it seems as if the person or object is moving.

4. Review what a biography is.

 Assessment: Share ideas about why Mickey has been popular for so long and about favorite present day cartoon characters. Pass the flip books around the class so each student sees several. Group students to give oral presentation and score it on organization.

Mickey Mouse Student Handout

Name _____ Date _____

1. Mickey Mouse has been a favorite cartoon character for over 75 years. What do you think it is about Mickey that has made children and grown-ups like him for so long?

_____

_____

_____

_____

2. Who is your favorite cartoon character? Describe him or her in a few sentences here.

_____

_____

_____

_____

_____

_____

3. Cartoons, like the ones that show Mickey Mouse, are made in a very simple way. Several pictures of Mickey are recorded. In each picture, Mickey looks like he has moved a very little bit from the last picture. When the pictures are flipped through quickly, it seems that Mickey is moving. Cut three pieces of drawing paper into four pieces each. Make sure all the pieces are the same size and shape. Put them together and staple one side to make a little book. On the front of each page of the book, draw a person. In each picture make it seem like the person has moved just a little. Flip through the pages of the book. It should seem like the person is really moving.

4. Time to create your own cartoon character. Think of a two word name where both words start with the same letter like Mickey Mouse or Daffy Duck. On another piece of paper, write a story about your character's life, a biography, and draw his or her picture. Tell the character's name, birthplace, favorite things your character likes to do, and anything else you think would help people get to know your character. Practice reading the biography out loud so you can introduce your character to your class.

Assignment 10 | The Mayflower

Skills: critical thinking; graphic organizer: chart; art: drawing; writing: fiction

 Th e Mayflower Background for Teachers

- The Mayflower left England on September 16, 1620, headed for Virginia, with 102 passengers aboard. It took two months to make the trip, and the ship got off course ending up farther north than planned, off the coast of what we now call New England.

- On November 21, 1620, the Mayflower anchored off Cape Cod, Massachusetts.

- Before anyone left the ship, the Pilgrims signed the Mayflower Compact establishing a government for the colony they were about to establish. While the ship remained anchored, a party of men explored the region to choose a suitable place to settle. On December 21, the Pilgrims left their ship to establish Plymouth Colony, the first permanent settlement in New England.

- The celebration of Thanksgiving Day in America goes back to colonial days. A year after the Pilgrims landed, in 1621, Governor William Bradford proclaimed a day for giving thanks and praying in gratitude for their first harvest.

The Mayflower Activities

1. Discuss the reasons for the Pilgrims' voyage to the New World.

2. Compare the duration of the trip (two months) with how quickly ships cross the ocean today (two or three days), and the reasons (sails versus steam engines).

3. Have the students imagine that they are going to a strange land where they do not know what to expect. Make a list of things they think would be important to have.

✓ **Assessment:** Divide the class into small groups to compile their lists of necessities into one list per group. As a class, compare the list of what the Pilgrims would have needed with the present day list compiled in class during the pre — assignment activities. Compare what Pilgrim children might have done to what present day children would do on a long voyage and discuss which workers would be most helpful when establishing a settlement. Post the ship pictures. Pair students to read stories and score the written composition on creativity.

The Mayflower Student Handout

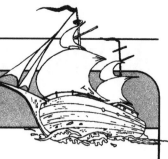

Name _____ Date _____

1. The Mayflower was a small ship. It carried 102 passengers and took two months to cross the Atlantic Ocean. If you were on a small ship for two months, what would you do to keep busy?

_____

_____

What do you think Pilgrim children did during their two – month trip?

_____

_____

2 What do you think the Pilgrims brought with them for the long trip and to start the settlement when they reached the New World? Make a list of all the things you think they would have needed.

_____

_____

_____

3 You need people who can do many different jobs when setting up a new settlement. If you were going to start a new settlement far from any other people, what kinds of workers would you want? For instance, you would need a doctor and a carpenter.

On the back of this paper make a chart showing the workers you would choose and why they would be the most important people to have.

4 Have you ever seen a ship in a bottle? You are going to make your own kind of ship in a bottle now. Look in an encyclopedia or other book and find a picture of the Mayflower. From a piece of cardboard, cut a bottle shape. On the shape draw and color a picture of the Mayflower. Cover the bottle shape with clear plastic wrap or cellophane.

5 Suppose you were on the Mayflower. You've left your friends and you're on your way to a new country and a new life. You have no idea what you will find when your trip is over. On another piece of paper, write a story about a person your age and his or her family who are on the Mayflower. How are they feeling? Do they have worries? Plans?

What will they do when they finally land?

Assignment 11 | Pinocchio

Skills: critical thinking; geography; writing: autobiography; art: puppets; oral presentation

Pinocchio Background for Teachers

- In 1882, the story of a wooden puppet who wanted to be human was published in Italy. Written by Carlo Lorenzini, better known as Carlo Collodi, the story of Pinocchio was translated into English in 1892, two years after the author's death.

- The story is about a shoemaker, Geppetto, who wanted a real live boy. He gets his wish and Pinocchio, a wooden puppet, comes to life. Unfortunately, Pinocchio is a very naive and innocent youngster who listens to every prankster who comes along, ignoring the admonitions of his conscience, the Cricket. Of course he gets into a lot of interesting troubles, and he cannot lie his way out of them because each time he tells a lie, his nose grows longer. It's a delightful story enjoyable for both children and adults.

- In 1940 Pinocchio was made into an animated motion picture by Walt Disney. The movie won Academy Awards for the musical score and the song "When You Wish Upon a Star."

Pinocchio Activities

1. Read Pinocchio or excerpts from it to the students. Discuss fiction and nonfiction. Could this story be true?

2. Discuss why lying is not a good thing to do. Perhaps the students would like to share what happened when they got caught in a lie.

3. Tell students that, while a biography is a story about someone's life, an autobiography is the life story that a person writes about himself.

 Assessment: Have a class discussion on what a conscience is and whether it's smart to listen to it. Discuss answers to the geography and math questions. Divide the class into small groups so that the puppets can share their autobiographies. Score the oral presentation on pacing.

Pinocchio Student Handout

Name _____ Date _____

1. Pinocchio was a wooden puppet who came to life. He was always getting into trouble because he lied and made bad choices. Cricket tried to get him to do the right thing, but Pinocchio did not always listen. Cricket was Pinocchio's conscience.

   What do you think a conscience is?

   _____

   _____

   _____

   Was there ever a time when your conscience told you not to do something? What happened?

   _____

   _____

   _____

1. *Pinocchio* was written in 1882 by a man called Carlo Collodi who lived in Italy.

   A. Find Italy on a map and answer these questions.
      What does its shape remind you of? _____
      What body of water surrounds it? _____
      What country is north of Italy?_____

   B. *Pinocchio* was translated into English from the Italian language in 1892.
      How many years was this after Mr. Collodi wrote the book? _____
      The author died two years before the book was translated. What year was that? _____

3. Puppets can be made of many different materials. They can be wood, like Pinocchio, or made from cloth, paper, cardboard, plastic, Popsicle sticks, or even from a glove, or an old sock.

   Think of a character from a story you have read or make up an interesting character. Choose any material you wish and make a puppet of the character you have chosen.

   On another piece of paper, write the story of your character's life as if he is writing it. This will be his autobiography and he will share it with some of your classmates.

Assignment 12 | Game Time

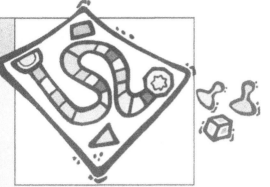

Game Time Background for Teachers

- Familiar with "Barrel of Monkeys," "Operation," "Battleship?" They, along with hundreds of other games and puzzles, are products of the Milton Bradley Company.

- Milton Bradley was born on November 11, 1836. In the early 1860s, he made a game called "The Checkered Game of Life." He successfully marketed the game and went on to form the Milton Bradley Company. Games from his company have been very popular and to this day children and adults enjoy Milton Bradley games and puzzles.

- Games have been played for thousands of years by people all over the world. The earliest games were probably played by people drawing game boards in the dirt with a stick. About 5000 years ago, people started making game boards from dried mud or wood, but there was no way to buy the games ready made. Everybody had to make their own boards and pieces so all games were not played exactly the same way. It was not until the eighteenth century, during the Industrial Revolution, that games could be mass produced with set rules and pieces.

- With the advent of computer games, more sophisticated games came into being using complex graphics and movie – like animation.

Game Time Activities

1. Discuss how games developed from simple games to sophisticated computer games.

2. Discuss students' favorites games and reasons why they are favorites.

3. Schedule two periods where students can play games: one for an outside active game and one for quiet games in the classroom.

Assessment: Share the sequence of events. Partner the students to share their game directions and the essays. Have a class discussion on what makes games fun to play. Score the written assignment on organization.

Game Time Student Handout

Name _____ Date _____

1. Milton Bradley was a person who is famous for inventing many games. Starting with number one, number the following facts about this man in an order that makes sense.

   _____ His company makes many of the games we play today.

   _____ The first game Milton Bradley made was called "The Checkered Game of Life."

   _____ Milton Bradley was born on November 11, 1836.

   _____ After his first game was successful, Bradley formed his game company.

2. There are so many kinds of indoor games to play today: card games, board games, computer games. Choose a game you like to play. Pretend your teacher does not know how to play the game. Write the directions for how to play it here.

   _____

   _____

   _____

   _____

   _____

3. Think about an indoor game you like and now play. What makes the game fun? Make a list of things that make you like the game.

   _____

   _____

   _____

   _____

   _____

4. Games can be quiet activities or they can be action packed. What kind of game do you like best? Do you like to play quiet indoor games or would you rather play a game outside where you get to run and make noise? On a different piece of paper, write at least two paragraphs telling what kind of game you like best. Then tell what kind of a person your choice shows you are.

Chapter 4 | December

				1	2	3
4	5	6	7	8	9	10
11	12	13	14	15	16	17
18	19	20	21	22	23	24
25	26	27	28	29	30	31

DECEMBER

Assignment 13 | Animals in Winter

Skills: science: migration, hibernation, body temperatures; critical thinking; reference: encyclopedia; writing: fiction

Animals in Winter Background for Teachers

- There are two main ways animals prepare themselves for winter. Warm-blooded animals (animals whose temperature is not dependent on the outside temperature) hibernate when the weather turns cold and food is scarce. Their body temperature falls and remains lower than normal while they are inactive. This period of inactivity can be from three to five months and, in extremely cold regions like Alaska, up to seven months.

- Brown bears and some smaller animals go into a deep sleep. Their body temperature drops just a little so they can wake up at times and feed or give birth and then resume their winter sleep.

- Amphibians and reptiles are cold-blooded (animals whose body temperature corresponds to the temperature of the air around them), so their winter sleep is not called hibernation although they do enter a lethargic state for the winter months.

- Another way animals avoid winter is through migration. In the autumn birds migrate to warmer climates and then return in spring. Even whales migrate, going from sub-polar waters to tropical seas in the autumn to give birth. Then, in the spring, they return to colder water which, very often, is richer in food.

Animals in Winter Activities

1. Discuss how winter weather affects food sources for wild animals.

2. Discuss whether students have seen flocks of birds in the sky. Talk about migration.

2. Discuss what hibernation means and how animals "sleep" through the winter.

 Assessment: Share the reasons for migration and hibernation and the answers to the questions about body temperatures. Pair the students to share stories and score the stories on mechanics.

Animals in Winter Student Handout

Name _____ Date _____

1. Many animals who live in cold places either hibernate or migrate for the winter.
Hibernate means animals sleep through the winter.
Migrate means they move to a warmer place for the winter.
Why do you think animals hibernate or migrate during winter?

_____

_____

2. Bears are animals that hibernate through the winter. Look in the encyclopedia and find out how bears hibernate.

_____

_____

3. Birds who live in colder places migrate every fall to warmer places and come back in the spring. Whales migrate too, just like birds. Look up whales in the encyclopedia and find out why and how they migrate.

_____

_____

4. Animals known as mammals are warm-blooded. Warm-blooded means that their body temperature stays the same whether it's hot or cold outside. So, if the temperature outside is 50 degrees, will the temperature of warm-blooded animal go down to 50 degrees too? Circle one answer: Yes   No

Amphibians and snakes are cold-blooded. That means their body temperature changes with the temperature around them. So, if the temperature outside is 50 degrees, will their temperature be around 50 degrees too? Circle one answer   Yes   No

People are mammals. Are you (circle one answer) cold-blooded or warm-blooded? What is the normal temperature of a person? _____
When can the temperature of a person change?

_____

5. Birds migrate together in flocks. What would happen if, during migration, a baby bird got lost? On another piece of paper, tell the story of the baby bird. How does it feel? Does it find its family? Does it have to find other birds to be with? What happens to it?

Assignment 14 | At the North and South Poles

Skills: graphic organizer: Venn Diagram; art: drawing; geography;
reference: encyclopedia; writing: essay

At the North and South Poles Background for Teachers

- Santa Claus may or may not live at the North Pole, but, if he does, he has plenty of company. Polar bears, large white bears that are the only marine bear, are found on the sea ice of the Arctic. Their diet consists of some of the animals that live in the region such as seals, walruses, whales, mussels, and kelp, as well as berries when available. Other animals that live in the North Pole region are musk ox, reindeer, caribou, fox, hare, wolf, lemming, and insects. The North Pole is the earth's most northern point. Temperatures in the North Pole are warmer that those at the South Pole.

- The South Pole is the southernmost point of the earth. Ninety percent of the world's ice covers Antarctica, the continent that is at the South Pole. Animals native to the region are penguins, birds, whales, porpoises, seals, and insects.

- While native peoples live at and around the Arctic Circle, the only people who live on Antarctica are scientists who are there to study the region.

- Glaciers (large masses of moving ice) are common in both areas as well as icebergs, pieces of ice that break off the glaciers and float away.

At the North and South Poles Activities

1. Locate the Poles on a globe.

2. Start a KWL chart for both the Arctic and the Antarctic. The first column in each chart will be what they already <u>know</u>. The second column will be <u>what</u> questions they have about the areas. The third column will be what they <u>learn</u> doing this project and will be filled in when the project is complete.

3. Review or teach how a Venn diagram is constructed.

 Assessment: Fill in the third column of the learning chart. Share the Venn diagrams. Post the animal pictures. Pair the students to share the essay and score it on content.

At the North and South Poles Student Handout

Name _____ Date _____

1. The Arctic Circle is at the North Pole and the Antarctic Circle is at the South Pole. Many animals live around both the Arctic Circle and the Antarctic Circle.

   Arctic Circle: polar bears, oxen, reindeer, caribou, fox, hare, wolves, whales, porpoises, seals, birds, insects.

   Antarctic Circle: penguins, birds, seals, porpoises, whales, insects.

   Polar bears live only in the Arctic.

   Penguins live only in the Antarctic.

   Draw a Venn Diagram. In one half show the animals that live in only in the Arctic. In the other half show the animals that live in the Antarctic. In the middle part show animals that live in both places.

2. Look in the encyclopedia and find pictures of animals that live at the North and South Poles. Pick one animal from each place and draw and color them on the back of this paper. Write their names and where they live under your pictures.

3. Look at a map or globe and find the North Pole and the South Pole. Which pole has more countries nearby? _____

   Name four of the countries near that pole.

   1. _____   4. _____

   2. _____   5. _____

4. Both the North Pole (Arctic Circle) and the South Pole (Antarctica) are covered by ice. Both places are very cold, but the Arctic is warmer than the Antarctic. People live in the Arctic, but only scientists visit the Antarctic. There are many animals in both places.

   Would you rather visit the North Pole or the South Pole? On another piece of paper, write at least two paragraphs to tell which one you would choose and why you would choose it.

Assignment 15 | Let's Draw

Skills: math: geometric shapes; art: drawing; oral presentation

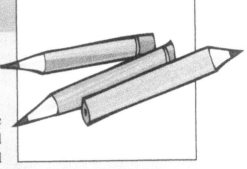

Let's Draw Background for Teachers

- Winter is a good time to practice sketching. The trees are bare and easier to sketch than trees in full bloom. Snow covered mountains, winter time activities like skiing, sledding, and building snowmen lend themselves to sketching.

- Sketching is an important activity for young students. It serves as a creative outlet, teaches patience, and increases the powers of observation by requiring students to inspect objects closely in order to sketch them accurately.

- Using number 2 lead pencils on white drawing paper gives a good result.
  The only directions students need are:
    - to sketch a picture that is as true-to-life as possible;
    - to take their time observing what they see in a scene or a still life before they begin;
    - to sketch in the background of the picture first;
    - to sketch lightly at first; and
    - to use the side of the pencil point to shade in darker areas of the drawing.

Let's Draw Activities

1. Show some black and white sketches to the students.

2. Talk about the directions listed above and demonstrate how to shade in a picture.

3. Look at a scene out the window or at a still life grouping you have made and list everything they see. If time allows, practice sketching in class.

4. Distribute several sheets of white drawing paper.

✔ **Assessment:** Discuss whether shading the shapes made a difference. Divide the class into small groups for the presentations. Post the sketches after the presentations. Score the oral presentation on organization.

Let's Draw Student Handout

Name _____ Date _____

1. A. Practice sketching basic shapes. Pencil them lightly at first, then darker when you
   have them the way you want them.

   Circle   Square   Rectangle   Triangle   Ellipse

   B. After you have drawn the shapes, try using the side of the pencil lead to shade in one
   side of the shapes. Shade darker at one side and get lighter as you get to the middle
   of the shape. What does shading do to the shapes?

   _____

   _____

2. Look around your home, in the yard or street, and choose a scene to sketch. Take your
   time observing everything, even the smallest things, in the scene. When you start, begin
   with what is in the background first, then draw what is closest to you. Use a number 2
   pencil and a piece of white drawing paper. Use your pencil to shade in the darker parts
   of your picture.

3. Now put a few things on a table for a still life. You might put a pitcher and a bowl, or a
   bowl filled with fruit, or a pair of shoes. Use anything you like that looks good to you.
   Before you start drawing, look at what you have set up carefully. Notice everything that is
   there. Draw the background first and then what is closest to you. Use a number 2 pencil and
   a piece of white drawing paper. Use your pencil to shade in the darker parts of your picture.

4. Some people find sketching very easy, while other people think it is very hard. What about
   you? What do you think? On another piece of paper, write at least two paragraphs telling what
   you like or don't like about sketching. What was hard for you? What was easy? Practice
   reading what you have written out loud so you can share your thoughts with the class.

Assignment 16 | The Brothers Grimm

Skills: graphic organizer: story chart; reference: dictionary; critical thinking; art: drawing; writing: description

Th e Brothers Grimm Background for Teachers

- Jacob and Wilhelm Grimm actually wrote many academic books including a German dictionary, but they are best known for their fairy tales, a compilation of old German folktales like *The Brementown Musicians*, *Briar Rose*, and *Sleeping Beauty*. They both spent many years teaching at the University of Berlin.

- In folklore, fairies are believed to be small creatures who look human and live in surroundings that are just like those where humans live. Good fairies are thought to be playful creatures who, while kind to humans, may also trick them. The tricks of bad fairies are not so playful. These include bewitching children, substituting an ugly fairy baby for a human baby — a changeling — and killing cattle. Brownies, gnomes, elves, goblins, trolls, and pixies are all enchanted creatures, and they all differ from one another in some way.

- In 1937, Walt Disney produced his first feature length animated motion picture, a story from the Brothers Grimm fairy tales, *Snow White and the Seven Dwarfs*.

The Brothers Grimm Activities

1. Read some of the Grimm fairy tales to the students and ask them to comment on the human characteristics found in the tales: jealousy, greed, helpfulness, love, fear, etc.

2. Use one of the fairy tales to teach a lesson on identifying main characters, setting, and summarizing the plot line.

3. Talk about any movies of the fairy tales the students may have seen. Did they like them? Why or why not?

 Assessment: Divide class into small groups to discuss story charts. As a class, share the definitions of the fairy-like creatures and the importance of knowing about their differences when writing about them. Post the pictures and score the description of what is in the picture on content-does it accurately describe what is in the picture?

The Brothers Grimm Student Handout

Name _____ Date _____

1. Tell about a fairy tale you have read by filling in the chart below.

Title:
a) Who is the main character, the person the story is mostly about?
b) What does main character look like? What kind of a person is he or she?
c) Describe the setting, where the story happens.
d) What is the problem?
e) How is the problem solved?

2. There are many kinds of fairy like creatures written about in stories. Each creature is different from the other in some way. Use a dictionary to find out about these creatures.

Brownies _____

Gnomes _____

Elves _____

Trolls _____

Pixies _____

If you were writing a fairy story, why would it be important to know how these creatures are different? Write your answer on the back of this paper.

3. Pick one part of the fairy tale you wrote about in number one. On another piece of paper, draw a picture of that part of the story. Under the picture, tell what is happening in the picture.

Chapter 5 | January

JANUARY						
1	2	3	4	5	6	7
8	9	10	11	12	13	14
15	16	17	18	19	20	21
22	23	24	25	26	27	28
29	30	31				

Assignment 17 | Snow, Hail and Sleet

Skills: graphic organizer: chart; critical thinking; science: clouds, precipitation, water cycle; writing: fiction; art: drawing

Snow, Hail and Sleet Background for Teachers

- Winter weather can bring several different kinds of precipitation.

- Rain occurs in all seasons. Water evaporates from warm bodies of water or wet land and travels up through the air. The water vapor condenses into clouds, then falls back to earth as rain.*

- Snow is the favorite precipitation of wintertime — at least for children and ski buffs. Ice crystals, not rain drops, form when water vapor condenses at temperatures that are below freezing. Snow crystals are six-sided and they appear white because they have a large number of surfaces to reflect light.

- Hail, an interesting phenomenon to observe but not to be caught in, occurs at the beginning of thunderstorms when the ground temperature is above freezing. Pellets of ice and snow are whirled upward in cumulonimbus clouds** and attach themselves to one another. Some can grow as large as five inches. When the pellets become too heavy for air currents to carry them, they fall to earth.

- Sleet is partially frozen rain. As rain falls, it enters a very cold layer of air close to the earth and freezes. Not all of it freezes though, so sleet is often a combination of frozen rain, rain, and snow crystals.

* All clouds are important parts of the water cycle. As water evaporates from the earth it travels to the upper atmosphere and condenses into clouds as tiny water droplets or ice crystals. Finally the water returns to earth as precipitation, and the cycle continues.

**Cumulonimbus or thunderhead clouds can extend from one mile to eight miles above the earth. They are dark and heavy with flat bottoms and high and rounded tops. They seem to rise like a mountain and indicate there will be heavy abrupt showers with thunder.

Snow, Hail and Sleet Activities

1. Discuss students' experiences with rain, snow, sleet, and hail. Ask if they know how each is formed and go over the explanations to make sure they understand.

2. Stock the classroom library with fiction and non-fiction books about winter.

3. Discuss fun winter activities that depend on the weather. (skiing, sledding, ice skating, snow shoeing, building snowmen, etc.)

4. Demonstrate how to construct a chart as asked for in the student handout.

 Assessment: Share precipitation charts and the pictures of the water cycle. Pair the students and have them show their drawings and read their stories to each other. Score the stories on creativity.

Snow, Hail and Sleet Student Handout

Name _____ Date _____

1. Water from the earth evaporates and rises to form clouds. Then the water vapor in the clouds comes back to earth in different forms.

   Raindrops are water droplets.
   Sleet is frozen rain that falls along with snowflakes and rain.
   Snowflakes are ice crystals with six sides.
   Hailstones are pellets of ice.

Make a chart that gives the name, season, and description of rain, sleet, snow, and hail.

Name	Season	Description

2. Rain, sleet, snow, and hail can cause problems for people. What are some problems that they can cause?

   Rain: _____

   _____

   Sleet: _____

   _____

   Snow: _____

   _____

   Hail: _____

   _____

3. Clouds are an important part of what we call the water cycle. Water evaporates from the earth, rises to make clouds, then drops to the earth from the clouds as rain or snow or sleet or hail. This happens over and over and over again. On the back of this paper, draw a picture that shows how the water cycle happens.

4. There are so many different things to do in winter. What are your favorites? Do you like to sled, ski, build snowmen, have a snowball fight, or sit by a warm fire, drinking hot chocolate and reading a book? On another piece of paper, write a story about some people who are having winter fun doing what you like to do best. Draw a picture to go with your story.

Assignment 18 | Gold!

Skills: critical thinking; writing: sequencing, essay; art: diorama; health: self knowledge

 ## Go Id! Background for Teachers

- Can you imagine the excitement that James Marshall felt when he found gold as he and John Sutter built a sawmill in the Sacramento Valley of California in January of 1848? The news was kept quiet until May of 1848 when a shopkeeper named Samuel Brannan stocked his store near Sutter's mill with mining equipment and supplies and went to San Francisco to spread the news. He made a fortune in the ensuing gold rush.

- San Francisco became almost a ghost town; many boats filled with gold seekers sailed up the Sacramento River. The mother lode, or main vein of gold, ran through the Sierra Nevada Mountain Range with La Porte as its northern boundary and Mariposa as its southern boundary. By 1849 gold seekers, called forty-niners or Argonauts, were coming from all over the United States as well as from Europe, Australia, and China.

- There were three routes from the eastern part of the United States. The least expensive was over land to California. Two other methods involved boats: take a boat to Panama, trek across that country, and take another boat up to San Francisco, or sail around Cape Horn, the southernmost point of South America.

- By 1852, over 200,000 forty-niners had reached California.

Gold! Activities

1. On a map, find the places in California where gold was discovered.

2. On a map, trace the three routes forty-niners took to California. Discuss the advantages and disadvantages of each.

✓ **Assessment:** Discuss personality types emphasizing the fact that there is no perfect type; each person's individuality is respected. Group the students to share the sequence of events the students chose and their essays. Display the dioramas. Score essay on organization.

Gold! Student Handout

Name _____ Date _____

1. A man named James Marshall was helping John Sutter build a sawmill in California. A sawmill is a place where you can cut logs. Think how excited he was when, as he was working, he discovered gold. Imagine you are James Marshall. What are the first three things you would do?

   First I would _____

   _____

   Then I would _____

   _____

   Finally I would _____

   _____

2. Make a diorama of James Marshall discovering gold at Sutter's Mill.

3. After gold was found at Sutter's Mill, many people from all over the world went to California to try to get rich. What kind of people do you think would leave family and friends behind and go search for gold miles away from where they lived?

   _____

   _____

   _____

   _____

   _____

   _____

   _____

4. If you had lived at the time of the Gold Rush, would you have left your home to search for gold?

   Circle   Yes   or   No.

   What do you know about yourself that made you answer the way you did? On another piece of paper, write at least two paragraphs that tell why you would or would not have left your home to search for gold.

Assignment 19 | Winnie the Pooh

Skills: health: self knowledge; writing: fiction; art: drawing

Wi)nnie the Pooh Background for Teachers

- Alan Alexander Milne, who wrote many books and plays for adults, probably never thought he would become famous for the books he wrote for his son, Christopher Robin. The two poetry books he wrote for Christopher were *When We Were Young* in 1924 and *Now We Are Six* in 1927. The other two books were stories about his son and his stuffed bear, Winnie the Pooh: *Winnie the Pooh* in 1926 and *The House at Pooh Corner*, 1928.

- Piglet, Kanga, Roo, Eeyore, Tigger, Rabbit, and Owl are the other characters that bring the Pooh stories to life.

- A. A. Milne was born on December 18, 1882 and died in 1956.

- Teddy Bears came into being in the United States in the early 1900's. In 1902, President Theodore Roosevelt went on a hunting trip and freed a black bear he had captured. After a cartoon showing this was published, a man named Morris Michtom asked the President if he could call the stuffed bears he made "Teddy." That was a nickname for the President. The President agreed and that was the beginning of the stuffed teddy bears that are so loved by children everywhere.

Winnie the Pooh Activities

1. Read some of Milne's work to the students, poems as well as stories. Discuss why they like or do not like what you have read. Who are their favorite characters? Least favorite?

2. Ask the students if they have ever had a favorite teddy bear and talk about why they were so dear to them.

 Assessment: Discuss favorite toys, story endings, and abc order. Divide the class into small groups so they can share their stories. Score the written assignment on neatness.

Winnie the Pooh Student Handout

Name _____ Date _____

1. A. A. Milne wrote stories for his son, Christopher Robin. The stories were about Christopher's favorite bear, Winnie the Pooh. If someone were to write a story about you and your favorite toy, what toy would the story be about?

   _____

   Why would it be about that toy? _____

   _____

2. Here are two stories about children and their favorite toys, but they have no ending. Can you write a few sentences to finish the stories?

   a) Lisa couldn't find her doll, Amy. She looked in the dollhouse. She looked on the shelf. She looked under the bed, but all she found down there was the dog's bone. That gave her an idea.

   _____

   _____

   _____

   _____

   b) Josh played with his big red fire truck every day. He liked to race it across the room so it crashed into the wall with a big bang. One day he tried to roll it on the floor, but it wouldn't move.

   _____

   _____

   _____

   _____

3. There are many different animals in the Winnie the Pooh books: a bear, a pig, kangaroos, a donkey, a tiger, a rabbit, and an owl. On the back of this paper, draw and label pictures of all the animals in ABC order. You will start with a bear and end with the tiger.

4. Many people like to read stories about animals. Some stories are about real live animals, some are about toy animals, and some are about imaginary animals that can be nice, or scary, or funny. On another piece of paper, write a story about an animal you like to read about. In the first part of the story, tell what the animal looks like and acts like too. Then, in the second part, tell about a problem the animal has. In the last part, tell how the animal solves the problem.

Assignment 20 | The Origin of the U.S.A. Flag

Skills: reference: encyclopedia; geography: states; critical thinking;
art: drawing; oral presentation

The Origin of the U.S.A. Flag Background for Teachers

- Even though some historians say it isn't true, most Americans believe that Betsy Ross made the first flag for the United States of America.

- Betsy Ross was born on January 1,1752. She was an expert seamstress who had an upholstery shop at 329 Arch St., Philadelphia, Pennsylvania.

- The story goes that when Congress appointed a committee to have a flag designed and made, George Washington, Robert Morris, and Colonel Ross decided that Betsy was the person for the job. They gave her a sketch of a proposed design for the flag, but it was Betsy who thought of making the stars five pointed. The flag was adopted in 1777.

- The first flag had 13 stars and stripes standing for the 13 original colonies that formed the new country. The number of stripes remains the same while the stars have grown to 50.

The Origin of the U.S.A. Flag Activities

1. Display pictures of the first flag and of subsequent flags up to the present flag. These can usually be found in the encyclopedia. Discuss the reasons behind the first design and the reasons for the changes through the years.

1. Compare our flag to those of other countries. Are there any commonalities such as color or symbols? What makes those colors or symbols so popular? Why are some not so common?

1. If the class were to design a class flag, what symbols and colors might the students want on it?

1. Distribute a piece of drawing paper for the flag they will design.

✓ **Assessment:** Share the year states were admitted to the union and the reason for stars being popular symbols. Discuss Betsy Ross' part in making the first flag. Divide the class into small groups for oral presentation and score it on creativity. Post the flags.

The Origin of the U.S.A. Flag Student Handout

Name _____ Date _____

1. The first United States flag that was adopted in 1777 had 13 stripes and 13 stars. They stood for the 13 states that made up the country at that time. Thirty – seven more states have joined the United States since then. That makes 50 states in all with 50 stars on the flag.

   Look up your state in the encyclopedia. What year did it become a state? _____

   Now look at all the states that touch your state. List them here and tell what year they became states.

   _____

   _____

   _____

   _____

   _____

1. Look at flags of other countries in an encyclopedia. You will see that many flags have stars on them. Why do you think a star is used on so many flags?

   _____

   _____

1. Most people believe that Betsy Ross made the first United States flag. Look up Betsy Ross in the encyclopedia. Find two things about her that would make you believe she could have made the first flag.

   _____

   _____

   _____

1. On another piece of paper, design a flag for your family. Think about these questions. Then decide what pictures you will use to tell something about your family. How many people in your family? What does your family like to do? Do you have favorite colors or foods? What else is there about your family that you might want to show on the flag?

   After you have drawn and colored your family flag, write a few paragraphs telling why you drew the flag the way you did. Practice reading your words out loud so you can share them with your class.

Chapter 6 |February

			1	2	3	4
5	6	7	8	9	10	11
12	13	14	15	16	17	18
19	20	21	22	23	24	25
26	27	28				

Assignment 21 | Two Presidents

Skills: reference: encyclopedia; graphic organizer: chart; writing: essay

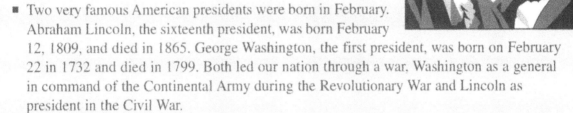

Two Presidents Background for Teachers

- Two very famous American presidents were born in February. Abraham Lincoln, the sixteenth president, was born February 12, 1809, and died in 1865. George Washington, the first president, was born on February 22 in 1732 and died in 1799. Both led our nation through a war, Washington as a general in command of the Continental Army during the Revolutionary War and Lincoln as president in the Civil War.

- George Washington was so honored that he is called the "Father of Our Country." When the war ended he could have been king, but he wanted a new type of government ruled by the people, not a king. He didn't want to serve as president, but he did because he felt the country needed him. He died only two years after leaving office.

- Abraham Lincoln loved to tell stories and play jokes. It is said he carried his letters and other papers in his tall stovepipe hat. At 6' 4" tall, he was our tallest president; he was also the first to be assassinated. In 1849, twelve years before he became president, he obtained a patent for a system to improve steamboats. While president he issued the Emancipation Proclamation, setting slaves free in rebelling states.

Two Presidents Activities

1. Read and discuss books about these two presidents.

2. Compare the two presidents: age when taking office and at death, marriage and children, place of birth, etc. Demonstrate making a chart with the comparisons.

3. Discuss alternatives to wars. Could Americans have won their independence or the union been saved in any other way?

 Assessment: Add the answers to numbers one and two to the classroom President chart. Discuss the information about the two wars on the student charts. Pair the students so they can read each other their ideas about being President of the United States. Score the essay on organization.

Two Presidents Student Handout

Name _____ Date _____

1. After the Revolutionary War, George Washington became the very first president of the United States of America. Look in the encyclopedia and find three things that you like about him. Write them here.

    1. _____

    2. _____

    3. _____

2. Abraham Lincoln was our sixteenth president. He was president during the Civil War. Look in the encyclopedia and find three interesting facts about him. Write them here.

    1. _____

    2. _____

    3. _____

3. The Revolutionary War and the Civil War are two important parts of the history of the United States.

    Fill in the chart below.

Name of War	Date Began and Ended	Who fought?
		against
		against

4. The job of being president of the United States can be very hard. Presidents have a lot of power, but they have to solve some very tough problems. George Washington did not want to be president, but he accepted the job because he felt the country needed him. Would you like to be President of the United States? Why or why not? Would you take the job even if you didn't want to if the country needed you? What would you do if you were President?

    On another piece of paper write at least two paragraphs answering these questions. Add anything else you wish to about being President of the United States.

Assignment 22 | U.S. Mail

Skills: geography; reference: encyclopedia; art: drawing; graphic organizer: graph; writing: letters

U.S. Mail Background for Teachers

- Benjamin Franklin is remembered for many things, including the fact that he is known as the "Father of the US Postal System." Franklin served the English government and the Continental Congress as a postmaster general. In 1789, President George Washington named the first postmaster general under the new Constitution, and Congress established postal rates in 1792.

- How many ways has the mail been carried? It has traveled by horse, by stage coach, steamship, railroads, trucks, airplanes, and, believe it or not, camels! Beginning in 1855 and lasting for a few years, camels carried the mail in the southwestern states. There is even one place today where mules carry the mail. Some Native Americans live under the south rim of the Grand Canyon and there is no other way to deliver the mail to them.

- An example of a stagecoach mail route is the Butterfield Stage Route between St. Louis, Missouri, and San Francisco, California, beginning in 1858. The trip took 25 days with stagecoaches traveling 24 hours a day stopping only to change horses or mules. The Pony Express was speedier than stagecoach, but lasted only 18 months.

- More information about postal history is available at http://www.usps.com.

U.S. Mail Activities

1. Discuss what the students know about the post office and all the ways mail has traveled in the United States. How else do we get news today? (e-mail, radio, television)

2. Review correct form for writing a letter.

3. Distribute a piece of graph paper.

 Assessment: Discuss order of sentences by date. Partner students to share their country and facts and compare mail graphs. If applicable to grade level, use results of mail graph to teach percentages. Post original commemorative stamps. Score letter on mechanics.

U.S. Mail Student Handout

Name _____ Date _____

1. In 1789 President George Washington named the first Postmaster General, the person in charge of the post office. Getting the mail to people all over the United States and the world has changed a lot since then. See if you can number the sentences about the post office in the right order. Start with number one for the sentence that should come first.

   _____ In 1792, Congress decided how much it would cost to send mail.

   _____ In 1789, President Washington named the first Postmaster General.

   _____ In 1858, stagecoaches carried the mail from Missouri to California in 25 days.

   _____ In 1855, camels carried the mail in the southwestern part of the United States.

2. People send letters all over the world. If you were a letter, where in the world would you want to be sent? Look at a map or a globe and pick a country that sounds exciting to you. Write the name of that country here and, in the encyclopedia, find three interesting facts about that country. Write them here.

   1. _____

   2. _____

   3. _____

3. In 1885, Congress honored George Washington, the Father of Our Country, and Benjamin Franklin, the Father of the US Post Office, by making stamps with their pictures on them. What person do you think should have a stamp made with his or her picture on it? Is it someone in your family, or a friend, or someone famous? Choose one person and, on the back of this paper, draw a stamp honoring that person. Then, in a few sentences, give the reason for your choice.

2. Some of the mail that comes to your house is business mail like bills or advertisements; some is personal like letters from family or friends. For three days, look at the mail that comes to your house and count the different kinds. How many bills and advertisements are there? How many letters or postcards are there? Then, on a piece of graph paper, make a bar graph to show how many of each there were.

4. Your teacher would like to know what you like best about school and what you like the least. On another piece of paper, write a letter to your teacher and tell about your favorite and least favorite school things. Remember to put the date on the top of the letter. Then write *Dear (your teachers name)*, and end the letter with something like *Your friend* or *Your student* and your name.

Assignment 23 | The Human Heart

Skills: science: circulatory system; health: lifestyle; reference: dictionary; writing: fiction

The Human Heart Background for Teachers

- The human heart is a pump made of muscle that pumps blood through the arteries and veins. Blood flows to the heart through the veins and away from the heart through the arteries. The heart beat is the sound of blood being pumped.

- The heart has four chambers. The two chambers at the top of the heart, the right atrium and the left atrium, hold blood coming into the heart and the two bottom chambers, right and left ventricles, hold blood leaving the heart. There are valves that open and close to let blood in and out of the chambers.

- Blood transports many things through the body. It brings oxygen and food to the cells and carries away waste products like carbon dioxide which is expelled from the body when we breathe out and waste to the kidneys that leaves the body as urine.

- Most heart attacks occur because narrowed blood vessels prevent blood from flowing freely to all parts of the body and to the heart. Fatty deposits from a poor diet, lack of exercise, and smoking are three causes for narrowed blood vessels. It is never too early or late to begin exercising, following a healthy diet, and shunning tobacco.

The Human Heart Activities

1. Show pictures of the circulatory system. Notice the different sizes of veins and arteries.

2. Have the students feel for their pulse on the wrist or just below the ear. Explain that when they feel the pulse they are feeling the heart pumping blood.

3. Ask the students to make a fist. That is about how big their heart is. Then have them tighten their fist and then loosen it. When the heart muscle tightens, blood flows out, and when it loosens, blood flows in. Ask: why does this make sense?

 Assessment: Divide the class into small groups so they can share their ideas on exercise and their stories. Show a picture of the heart so students can compare their drawings to it. Score the "heart" stories on content (accurate use of words).

The Human Heart Student Handout

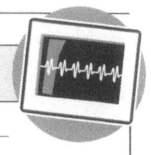

Name _____ Date _____

1. The heart has four chambers or rooms. There are two on top called the right atrium and the left atrium. They hold blood coming into the heart. There are two on the bottom called the right and left ventricles. They hold blood ready to go out of the heart.

   Draw a picture here of the four rooms of the heart. Label them.

2. Blood goes to the top part of the heart through veins.

   Blood leaves the bottom part of the heart through arteries.

   Look at the picture you drew of the heart. Add one vein going into the top of the heart. Add one artery coming out of the bottom of the heart. Label them.

3. Your heart is a muscle. If you exercise, it will be a strong muscle. Any exercise that makes the heart beat faster keeps it healthy.

   What are some things you can do to keep all your muscles strong?

   _____

   _____

   _____

4. The word "heart" is used to make many other words. On another piece of paper, draw and color the prettiest heart you can. Then look in a dictionary and find at least five words that begin with "heart" like "heartache." Under your picture, write a story that uses each of the words you found. Will your story be funny, or sad, or lovey-dovey for Valentine's day?

Assignment 24 | Groundhog Day

Skills: critical thinking; reference: dictionary; writing: fiction

Groundhog Day Background for Teachers

- Groundhog Day, February 2, is an unofficial holiday we celebrate in the USA.

- The woodchuck, known as a groundhog in the eastern states, is a rodent with a heavy body, short legs and ears, a flat head, and is gray or brown with its fur tipped with reddish or white hairs. It eats green vegetation like grasses. Starting in early fall, the groundhog hibernates through the winter months in its underground home which it has lined with grass. It closes up its den, curls itself into a ball, and settles in for a long winter's sleep.

- The myth goes that the groundhog rouses itself on February 2 and pops out of its hole to see if it's time to get moving again. If the day is cloudy and the groundhog cannot see its shadow, it decides winter is over and stays above ground. If, however, the day is sunny and it sees its shadow, there will be six more weeks of cold weather, and the little creature pops back into its den for a little more sleep.

- The most famous groundhog is Punxsutawney Phil from Punxsutawney, Pennsylvania. Thousands of people gather to watch men in formal top hats take Phil from his hole so that he can forecast the weather. *The Life and Times of Punxsutawney Phil* is a movie about Phil. Classroom activities that center around the day can be found at http://www.edhelper.com.

Groundhog Day Activities

1. Talk about rodents: woodchucks, rats, etc. and the myth about Groundhog Day.

2. Review hibernation. (See assignment 13)

 Assessment: Share opinions about Groundhog Day and book characters. Share definition of rodent and list all animals that are rodents. Group the students to share stories and score the written assignment on creativity.

Groundhog Day Student Handout

Name _____ Date _____

1. Groundhog Day is always on February 2. If the groundhog sees its shadow on that day, there will be six more weeks of winter. If it doesn't see its shadow, winter is over.

   Do you think this is true?

   Why or why not?

   _____

   _____

   _____

   _____

2. A groundhog or woodchuck is a rodent. So are mice and rats. Look up the word rodent in the dictionary and write what it means here.

   _____

   _____

   _____

3. There are many stories written about mice and rats. Templeton in *Charlotte's Web* was a rat, Stuart Little is a mouse who really gets around, Mickey and Minnie Mouse are mice made famous by Walt Disney, the mice in the movie of Cinderella helped her get to the ball. On the back of this paper, draw a picture of a mouse or rat who is in a book or story you have read. Under the picture tell if the rodent is a good or a bad character and why you think so.

4. Suppose the groundhog who comes out of his den on February 2 likes to play tricks on people. What might he do to fool everybody about winter? What problems could he make for people who were fooled? On another piece of paper, write a story about this groundhog and how he fooled everyone about whether winter was over or not.

Chapter 7 | March

			MARCH			
			1	2	3	4
5	6	7	8	9	10	11
12	13	14	15	16	17	18
19	20	21	22	23	24	25
26	27	28	29	30	31	

Assignment 25 | Dr. Suess

Skills: critical thinking; art: drawing; writing: fiction

Dr. Suess Background for Teachers

- A scholar, cartoonist, artist, author, Academy Award winner, and recipient of a Pulitzer Prize citation: introducing Theodor Seuss Geisel, better known as Dr. Seuss.

- Dr. Seuss was born in Springfield, Massachusetts on March 4, 1904. He attended Harvard College and Oxford University where he studied English Literature. After teaching himself to draw, he supported himself for almost ten years as a cartoonist.

- Then, in 1937, Dr. Seuss wrote and illustrated his first book, *And To Think That I Saw It On Mulberry Street.* It was a best seller, and he followed it with *King's Stilts* in 1939 and *Horton Hatches the Egg* in 1940. All in all, he wrote about 40 books.

- Dr. Seuss didn't limit himself to children's books. He wrote two books for adults as well as films for the war effort during World War II (1939-1945), winning an Academy Award for *Design for Death*, a documentary about the Japanese people. His second Academy Award was for creating the cartoon character Gerald McBoingBoing. In 1984, Dr. Seuss accepted a special Pulitzer Prize citation for his lifetime work of contributing to children's education and enjoyment.

Dr. Suess Activities

1. Build a classroom library of Dr. Seuss books. Start a bar graph with all the students' names, telling them to fill in a space on the graph over their name each time they read or someone reads them a Dr. Seuss book.

2. Make a list of characters from some of the Dr. Seuss books and talk about the students' favorites.

 Assessment: Divide the class into small groups to share their answers to questions 1 and 2 and their stories. List all the rhyming words on a chart for future reference. Score written assignment on mechanics.

Dr. Suess Student Handout

Name _____ Date _____

1. Dr. Seuss wrote about 40 books. Read some of those books or ask someone to read some to you. Which one is your very favorite? Why?

    _____

    _____

    _____

    _____

    _____

2. Dr. Seuss taught himself how to draw and worked drawing cartoons for almost 10 years before he wrote his books.

    Think about something that you cannot do like painting, or playing a certain game, or riding a skateboard. Could you teach yourself or would you need someone to teach you? On the back of this paper, draw a picture of yourself doing whatever it is you want to learn to do. Then, if you can teach yourself, tell how you will do that. If you can't teach yourself, tell why you need someone else to teach you.

3. Dr. Seuss' stories had many rhymes in them like cat and hat. Look through several of his books and make a list of other rhymes he used. Some of them may be nonsense words.

    _____

    _____

    _____

    _____

4. Cartoon characters can look as silly or as funny as you make them. Their names sometimes give us a hint about what they are like. For instance you just know from his name that the Grinch is not a nice person. Cartoon characters can be sweet, grumpy, or mean and nasty. They can like to have fun or always be getting into trouble.

    Make up your very own cartoon character. What will he or she look like? How will he or she act? On another piece of paper draw your character. Make up a name that gives us an idea of what your character is like. Then write a story that shows us the name is just right for the way he or she acts.

Assignment 26 | In Like a Lion

Skills: critical thinking; graphic organizer: Venn Diagram; writing: poem; oral presentation

In Like a Lion Background for Teachers

- In like a lion, out like a lamb, that's the month of March. That saying probably came about because when March begins, it is still winter, but spring comes on March 21, and we begin to see signs that the earth is awakening with budding trees and warmer days.

- March 21 is called the Vernal or Spring Equinox. On that day, there are 12 hours of day and 12 hours of night. The word equinox means equal night. On that day the sun is directly above the Equator and from then on, the northern hemisphere begins to tip more toward the sun bringing warmer weather.

- The lands around the Equator do not have seasons. They have mild weather all year long. A demonstration with the globe and a light source will show that that part of the earth is never tipped very much either toward the sun or away from it.

In Like a Lion Activities

1. Name the four seasons. Demonstrate the position of the earth in relation to the sun during each season. In winter, the northern hemisphere is tipped away from the sun; in spring the earth is at a right angle beginning to tip toward the sun. In summer the northern hemisphere is tipped toward the sun and, at the autumn equinox, again at a right angle starting to tip away from the sun starting the cycle over again. Use a flashlight or other light source as the sun and a globe.

2. As you demonstrate the changing of the seasons, point out the countries close to the equator and ask if the students think there is much change in temperature .

3. List the four seasons and the characteristics of each one.

4. Review how to make a Venn Diagram.

 Assessment: Share student's answers to the first three questions. Divide the class into small groups to share their poems. Score the oral presentation on pacing.

Answers to the jokes

a long March, spring forth, a Military March

In Like a Lion Student Handout

Name _____ Date _____

1. We often say that the month of March comes in like a lion and goes out like a lamb. What does the word lion make you think of? What do you think lambs are like?

   _____

   _____

   _____

   What other animals could be used instead of lion and lamb that would give the same meaning to the saying?

   _____

   _____

2. March begins in the winter but ends in the spring.

   There are some things you can only do in winter, and there are some things you can do only in spring and summer. There are also things you can do in both seasons.

   On the back of this paper, draw a Venn Diagram. On one side write winter things; on the other side write spring/summer things. In the middle, write things you can do all year long.

3. Here are some March jokes. Put two words together in the right order to answer each question.

   Military   long   March   forth   March   spring

   What is the worst month for someone who does not like to hike? a _____

   What is an order to get moving? _____

   What music does a soldier walk to? a _____

4. Some people have favorite seasons. Choose either Spring or Winter and write a free form poem about the season you choose. Write the name of the season on the first line, then make a list of what you like about that season and what you like to do at that time. Practice reading your poem so you can share it with the class.

   _____

   _____

   _____

   _____

   _____

Assignment 27 | Know Your State

Kn ow Your State Background for Teachers

- In 1776, when the United States won its freedom from Great Britain, there were 13 original states, all on the eastern seaboard: Connecticut, Delaware, Georgia, Maryland, Massachusetts, New Hampshire, New Jersey, New York, North Carolina, Pennsylvania, Rhode Island, South Carolina, and Virginia. As the settlers began to explore and move westward and the government bought land from foreign nations, more states joined the Union until the count reached 50 with the acceptance of Alaska and Hawaii in 1959.

- The order of states joining the Union demonstrates the westward movement across the continent although California, the first state on the Pacific Ocean, became a state in 1850, well before several states located farther east. All 48 contiguous states were part of the United States by 1912 with the addition of Utah, Oklahoma, New Mexico and Arizona in that year.

Know Your State Activities

1. Post a large map of the United States. Ask if any students have visited or lived in other states. Mark the states on the map with tiny post-its or dots and student name.

2. Have an informal question and answer period to see how much students know about your state and your neighboring states.

3. Post a map of your state. Talk about interesting trips students or you have taken within your state and locate them on the map.

4. Locate important rivers and national forests, parks, military bases, etc.

 Assessment: Post pictures of state. Discuss meaning of motto and reasons first thirteen colonies were on the east coast. Point out bordering states on US map and share capitals of your own state and the bordering states. Group students to share stories and score the written composition on content.

Know Your State Student Handout

Name _____ Date _____

1. Every state in the United States has a state flag, flower, animal, and motto.

   On the back of this paper, draw a picture of the shape of your state, marking and naming the capital city. Under that outline, draw the state flag, flower, and animal and write the motto of your state. Then write a few sentences about what you think the state motto means.

2. Look at a map. What states border your state? List them here and name their capitals.

   _____

   _____

   _____

   _____

3. The United States began with thirteen states in 1776. By 1912, the last four of the first 48 states were part of the United States: Utah, Oklahoma, New Mexico, and Arizona.

   What year did your state become a state? _____

   How about the states that border your state? When did they become states?

   _____

   _____

   _____

4. In 1776, the first 13 states were all up and down the eastern seacoast. Why do you think that is true? Hint: think about the first settlers.

   _____

   _____

   _____

5. Alaska and Hawaii were the last states to join the United States, both in 1959. They are both interesting and beautiful states to visit. Which one of those states would you like to visit? On another piece of paper, write a story about a person who gets to visit that state. Write about what they do there. Do they go sightseeing? Do they do a lot of swimming, surfing or skiing? Do they like it so much they move there? Look in the encyclopedia for some information about the state so you can write about real places and things to do.

Assignment 28 | Mars, Our Neighbor Planet

Skills: graphic organizer: Venn Diagram; science: planets; critical thinking; reference: encyclopedia; writing: fiction

Mars, Our Neighbor Planet Background for Teachers

- Mars is a planet so similar to Earth that for years people have wondered if there were other beings living there.

- Both Mars and Earth have polar ice caps, their days are almost the same with the day on Mars 37 and 1/2 minutes longer than that on Earth, and Mars tilts on its axis creating seasons just as on Earth. There are volcanoes on Mars, and one of them, Olympus Mons, is believed to be the largest in the solar system.

- There are many differences between Earth and Mars. Mars takes almost twice as long to orbit the Sun – 687 days to our 365, Mars has two moons, one more than Earth, and the seasons on Mars are twice as long as Earth's seasons. In addition, the atmosphere surrounding Mars is mainly carbon dioxide instead of oxygen, and the surface of Mars is very much like that of the Earth's moon.

- The United States and the USSR have sent several missions to explore Mars and bring back samples of earth and rocks from the planet hoping to discover whether life in any form ever existed on Mars. Exploration of the planet has not found any living organisms but, because of the discovery of river channels, scientists believed that maybe there once was life on the planet. In 2004, a European space probe revealed images that may show that a sea of ice exists close to the equator of Mars, increasing the possibility that microscopic life may be found there.

- Mars got its name and its nickname because it is covered with red dust. To the early discoverers of the planet, red was the color of blood reminding them that blood is shed during wars. Since the Roman god of war is Mars, that seemed an appropriate name. Observation of the red dust swirling in wind storms which are common on Mars led to its nickname, the "Red Planet."

Mars, Our Neighbor Planet Activities

1. Review the names and positions of the planets.

2. Tell the students how Mars got its name. Considering the red color of the planet, what other names could they suggest?

3. Tell the story of the radio show "The War of the Worlds." Orson Welles announced that the state of New Jersey was being invaded by Martians. The story was not true, but the people who were listening panicked. They rushed to escape from the Martian invasion. Ask why we could not be fooled that way now.

4. Teach or review how to make a Venn Diagram.

 Assessment: Share information from diagrams by making one on the board and filling in data from students. Discuss alternate names for planets. Divide the class into small groups to read their stories. Score written assignment on creativity.

Mars, Our Neighbor Planet Student Handout

Name _____ Date _____

1. The planet Mars and Earth are alike in many ways. Both Mars and Earth have polar ice caps, their days are almost the same length, Mars tilts on its axis creating seasons just as on Earth, and there are volcanoes on Mars and Earth.

   There are many differences between Earth and Mars. Mars takes 687 days to orbit the Sun; Earth takes 365. Mars has two moons; Earth has one. The seasons on Mars are twice as long as Earth's seasons. In addition, Mars is surrounded by carbon dioxide, Earth by oxygen.

   Make a Venn diagram showing how Earth and Mars are alike and different. The like things go in the middle of the diagram; the different things go on either side.

2. To date we know of at least nine planets. On the back of this paper, draw a picture of the solar system showing all the nine planets. Label them. If they have moons, show the moons too.

3. The planet Mars, the Red Planet, looks red because windstorms swirl its red dust up into the atmosphere. The first people to see it named it after the Roman god of war because the color reminded them of bloody battles. Pick one of the other planets. Read about that planet in the encyclopedia. Do you think its name is the best one for the planet? Think of another name for that planet. Why does your name fit the planet?

   _____

   _____

4. Suppose you went to Mars and you found something so amazing you almost couldn't believe it. Was it animal, vegetable, or mineral? Were you able to take it back to Earth? Was it scary? On another piece of paper, write the story of your trip to Mars.

Chapter 8 │ April

A	P	R	I	L		
						1
2	3	4	5	6	7	8
9	10	11	12	13	14	15
16	17	18	19	20	21	22
23/30	24	25	26	27	28	29

Assignment 29 │ National Poetry Month

Assignment 30 │ Earth Day

Assignment 31 │ Morse Code

Assignment 32 │ Aesop's Fables

Assignment 29 | National Poetry Month

Skills: critical thinking; writing: poetry; art: drawing

National Poetry Month Background for Teachers

- National Poetry Month, instituted by the Academy of American Poets in April, 1996, is held every April. The Academy works with other groups such as the NCTE, the American Library Association, and the office of the U.S. Poet Laureate to accomplish its goals which include making poetry an important part of school curriculum, encouraging an interest in poetry and poets, introducing Americans to the pleasure of reading poetry, and garnering support for our nation's poets. The Academy distributes posters free of charge to teachers, librarians and booksellers. More information is available at their website: http://www.poets.org/npm.

- Students usually enjoy the work of Shel Silverstein and Jack Prelutsky, but there are many other poets that will appeal to your students once they are introduced to their work. Include a wide variety of poets in your classroom library and look for poetry readings, book displays, and workshops in libraries and bookstores during the month.

National Poetry Month Activities

1. Read poems to the students every day and discuss the differences in form.

2. Try writing different kinds of poetry. *Rhyming couplet:* two lines that end in rhyming words. For example: Can you make a wish, On a flying fish? *Haiku:* captures a moment in time in a three line poem, usually with five syllables in the first and third lines and seven syllables in the second line. You can find books of haiku at the library to show examples. One is *Red Dragonfly on My Shoulder*, translated from the Japanese by Sylvia Cassedy and Kunihiro Suetake. (USA: HarperCollins Publishers, 1992)

 Assessment: Discuss what kind of reading the students prefer and share the "Jack and Jill" poems. Form small groups so the students can recite the poem they memorized. Score the oral recitation on eye contact. Post the color poems and score them on neatness.

National Poetry Month Student Handout

Name _____ Date _____

1. The month of April is National Poetry Month. It is organized to encourage people to read poetry. What do you like to read best, poetry or stories? _____

   Why do you like that kind of reading best?

   _____

   _____

   _____

   _____

2. The first poems you probably heard were nursery rhymes. They are usually simple rhyming poems. Here is "Jack and Jill" on one side of the page. On the other side, fill in the blanks with different names and activities. The rhythm will sound like "Jack and Jill" but it will be your very own poem. Remember to make up rhymes.

Jack and Jill	_____ and _____
Went up the hill	Went _____
To fetch a pail of water.	To _____.
Jack fell down	_____ _____ _____
And broke his crown	And _____
And Jill came tumbling after.	And _____.

3. Find a book of poems you like. Choose one poem, write its title and author here. Memorize it, or a part of it if it is very long. Practice saying it out loud with lots of expression.

4. Now you will write another poem. It is called a free verse color poem. This is a poem that has no rhyme and is about your favorite color. Keep writing lines until you can't think of any more things that remind you of your color. Here's an example.

   I like blue,
   The sky above,
   The roaring ocean,
   My teddy bear's eyes

   Write and illustrate your poem on another piece of paper.

Assignment 30 | Earth Day

Skills: art: poster; science: conservation; reference: encyclopedia; oral presentation

Earth Day Background for Teachers

- How did the first Earth Day come about? It was the brainchild of a very persistent and concerned person.

- In 1962, a group of United States senators headed by Senator Gaylord Nelson became concerned about the deteriorating environment of the country. They persuaded President Kennedy to take a tour around the United States to point out the serious state of our environment to the people of the country. The five-day tour in September of 1963 was unsuccessful in that it didn't arouse much attention or concern.

- Nelson, however, did not give up on his crusade for a cleaner environment. In 1969, he began raising money for a teach-in about the environment that was held in the spring of 1970. This was the first Earth Day.

- Since then, the idea of keeping our world a safer and cleaner place to live has resulted in recycling efforts, better environmental laws, and a national yearly Earth Day when awareness is raised as to what each individual can do to protect our world.

Earth Day Activities

1. Ask students to share what they have done on previous Earth Days or what they think they could do on the next Earth Day to make the world a cleaner and safer place to live.

2. List the students' ideas in a prominent place in the classroom with space for names after each item. Tell them that when they do one of the actions on the list they may write their name next to it.

3. Hand out large pieces of construction paper for conservation poster.

4. Talk about how to write and present a speech.

 Assessment: Post the posters. Divide the class into small groups for the oral presentation and for sharing how birds, worms, and trees help the environment. Score the oral presentation on eye contact.

Earth Day Student Handout

Name _____ Date _____

1. Everyone of us needs to be careful with how we use our earth's resources. List five ways you can help save our natural resources. Example: *you could be careful of how much water you use when you rinse dishes or brush your teeth.* On a piece of construction paper, draw a poster to illustrate one of your suggestions. Write the suggestion under the picture.

   1. _____

   2. _____

   3. _____

   4. _____

   5. _____

2. What is something you can do to celebrate Earth Day? Could you put food out for the birds? Could you collect aluminum cans and recycle them? Can you pick up any litter that you see around your home or school? Make a list of what you can do. If you do any of the things on your list, put a happy face next to it. You have helped the earth!

   _____   _____

   _____   _____

   _____   _____

   _____   _____

3. Our world is made up of many kinds of life, and they all help us in some way.

   How do birds help us? _____

   _____

   How do worms help us? _____

   _____

   How do trees help us? _____

   _____

   _____

4. It is very important that we tell other people about being careful with our earth and celebrating Earth Day. Write a short speech that tells how to keep our world clean and safe. Say your speech to your family and friends. You will say it to your class too.

Assignment 31 | Morse Code

Skills: critical thinking; writing: essay

Morse Code Background for Teachers

- Samuel Finley Breese Morse was born on April 27, 1791 and died in 1872.

- He was a successful painter and sculptor when he invented the telegraph in 1836 and obtained a patent for it in 1837. He received financial support from Alfred Vail who worked with Morse in developing the telegraph and the Morse Code.

- The Morse code uses a series of dots and dashes to send messages through the telegraph or by using some sort of light source.

- In 1843, Congress gave Morse $30,000 to establish a telegraph line from Washington DC to Baltimore, Maryland. On May 24, 1844, the first message was transmitted on that line: "What God hath wrought."

- In 1876, Alexander Graham Bell invented the telephone, a great improvement over the telegraph. Unlike the telegraph that needed trained operators to decode, record, and deliver messages, the telephone allowed people to speak to one another.

Morse Code Activities

1. Discuss the various ways we send messages today: telephone, cell phones, faxes, e-mail, snail mail.

2. What are some situations where we might use Morse code today? (For example, using a flashlight, we might be able to signal for help if lost. SOS would be three dots, three dashes and three more dots (..._ _ _...) with a dash held for three beats and a dot for one.)

3. Ask the children to practice sending the SOS signal. Dots can be a tap of a finger or pencil and a dash the drawing of a finger or pencil across a surface to a count of three.

4. You can also use a flashlight to practice the signal.

 Assessment: Share the answer to the coded message. Partner the students so they can try to break each other's code and decipher the word tapped in Morse Code. Score the essay on mechanics.

Answer to sentence in code

I scream, you scream, we all scream for ice cream

Morse Code Student Handout

Name _____ Date _____

1. Break the code! There is a hidden message written here. Each number represents a different letter of the alphabet. Can you read the message? Here's a hint. Z=26, Y=25, X=24, W=23.

   9   19-3-18-5-1-13,   25-15-21   19-3-18-5-1-13,   23-5   1-12-12
   19-3-18-5-1-13   6-15-18   9-3-5   3-18-5-1-13.

   Write the message here.

   _____

   _____

2. Design your own code using symbols or numbers, or by exchanging one letter for another. Write a short sentence using your code. Keep a copy of your code.

3. The Morse Code uses a combination of dots and dashes to represent letters and numbers.

   A._ B_... C_._. D_.. E. F.._. G__. H.... I.. J.___ K_._
   L._.. M__ N_. O___ P.__. Q__._ R._. S... T_
   U.._ V..._ W.__ X_.._ Y_.__ X_.._ Y_.__ Z__..

   Write a word in Morse Code. Practice the word by tapping for each dot and scraping your finger along a surface for each dash. Hold a dot for one beat and a dash for three beats. See if others can understand your word.

4. The Morse Code was named after Samuel Morse, its inventor. There are many places or things named after famous people. The sandwich was named after the Earl of Sandwich who first folded bread around a filling, Halley's comet after the man who discovered it, and Ronald Reagan International Airport in Washington, DC, named for a United States president.

   What would you like named for you? An invention, a new sports maneuver, a discovery of something in space? On a separate piece of paper, write an essay with at least two paragraphs telling how you would like to be remembered and the reasons for your choice.

Assignment 32 | Aesop's Fables

Skills: critical thinking; reference: dictionary; art: drawing; writing: fiction

Aesop's Fables Background for Teachers

- The first day of April is a day for fooling others, April Fool's Day. While a fable is a short story, usually about animals, that teaches a lesson, many of the stories also revolve around someone being tricked or fooled, making them a good topic for study during this month.

- Some of the most famous and well-read fables are those written by a freed Greek slave named Aesop, who lived in the sixth century BC. Because Aesop's stories were passed on in the oral tradition for a great many years, some people believe that Aesop, the man, never existed but was a legend attached to the fables. At any rate, the stories were written down by Greek and Roman writers at a much later date and attributed to Aesop.

- There are a great many stories credited to Aesop. The most familiar of these are probably the "Tortoise and the Hare," "The Mouse and the Lion," and " The Fox and the Grapes."

- All of Aesop's fables are quite short and lend themselves to interesting discussions about universal truths and the principles of good behavior.

Aesop's Fables Activities

1. Read a few of the fables to the students and discuss the moral taught.

2. Tell the story of Aesop and how his stories were passed down through the years in the oral tradition (word of mouth). Ask if any of the students know of stories passed down in their families by word of mouth. Share if they like.

Assessment: Share the lessons to be learned from the two fables and the definitions. Divide the class into small groups to share their original fables. Score the written assignment on neatness.

Definitions from student handout:

Legend: a story from the past having some historical basis

Myth: a story with historical basis explaining a belief or a practice

Saga: a story about historic or legendary figures of Norway and Iceland

Aesop's Fables Student Handout

Name _____ Date _____

1. A fable is a short story that tries to teach a lesson. A man named Aesop made up fables many years ago. One of his most famous fables is about a lion and a mouse. The lion helps the mouse and the mouse promises to help the lion one day. The lion laughs thinking a little mouse can never help a big strong lion. But one day the lion is caught in a net and the mouse chews at the net until the lion is free.

   What lesson do you think Aesop was trying to teach us in this fable?

   _____

   _____

   _____

   _____

   _____

2. A fable is just one kind of story that has been handed down through many years. Look in the dictionary and find out what these other kinds of stories are.

   legend _____

   _____

   myth _____

   _____

   saga _____

   _____

3. Another famous fable from Aesop is *The Tortoise and the Hare*. In this story, the tortoise and the hare have a race. Everyone knows the tortoise is very slow and a hare is very fast. So the hare decides to take a nap in the middle of the race, but the tortoise keeps going and wins the race. On the back of this paper, draw a picture of some part of the race. Write a few sentences below the picture to tell what is happening and what lesson we can learn from this story.

4. Fables are usually stories about animals, about things that really could not happen, and they teach a lesson. Now it's your turn to write a fable. What animals will you write about? What will they do that you know could really not happen? What lesson will we learn from the story? Write your story on another piece of paper. Draw a picture to go with your fable.

Chapter 9| May

MAY						
	1	2	3	4	5	6
7	8	9	10	11	12	13
14	15	16	17	18	19	20
21	22	23	24	25	26	27
28	29	30	31			

Assignment 33 | National Be Kind to Animals Week

Skills: critical thinking; writing: fiction; art: drawing

National Be Kind to Animals Week
Background for Teachers

- You would think that there wouldn't be any need for an organization that promotes being kind to animals. However, not all animals are treated with kindness and so there are several organizations that work to ensure all animals are treated humanely.

- Henry Bergh founded the American Society for the Prevention of Cruelty to Animals in 1866. It was the first organization of its kind in the United States. The Society works not only with house pets but also, through the years, has rescued and placed thousands of exotic pets with zoos or wildlife preserves. It also helped pass the first anti-cruelty law in the United States. Their website is http://www.aspca.org.

- In 1877, the American Humane Society came into being with the purpose of preventing cruelty and abuse toward animals and children. Their website is http://www.americanhumane.org. Both websites contain a lot of interesting information and news about upcoming events.

- The first week in May is "Be Kind to Animals Week." There may be days during that week with other names such as "Hug Your Cat Day" and "Mayday for Mutts."

National Be Kind to Animals Week Activities

1. Ask students to share how they take care of their pets.

2. Discuss what they could do if they saw someone mistreating an animal or other person.

3. Demonstrate how to draw a comic strip with several pictures in a row using bubbles to show what the characters are saying. Distribute a piece of drawing paper.

 Assessment: Divide class into small groups to share answers to first three questions. Pass comic strips around the class so each child sees at least three others. They may write a short comment on the back of the strip noting if they enjoyed it or have a suggestion on how it could be improved. Score comic strips on content.

National Be Kind to Animals Week Student Handout

Name _____ Date _____

1. The first week in May is "National Be Kind to Animals Week." Monday is sometimes called "Hug Your Cat Day." What would you call the other days of the week to tell people to show some act of kindness to their pets? Love your Lizard? Hold Your Hamster?

Sunday: _____

Monday: Hug Your Cat Day

Tuesday: _____

Wednesday: _____

Thursday: _____

Friday: _____

Saturday: _____

2. The American Society for Prevention of Cruelty to Animals and the American Humane Society are two groups that try to make sure that all animals are treated with kindness. What do you think happened that made people start these groups? What could they have seen or heard about?

_____

_____

_____

_____

3. Sometimes people do not know how to care for their pets in the best way. If you knew someone who did not know how to do this, what would you tell them? Make a list of all the things you can think of that people could do for their pets to keep them safe, healthy, and happy.

_____

_____

_____

4. Choose two of the ways people should care for their pets that you listed above. Make a comic strip showing people not doing the right thing and then using your rules. Show the people talking about what they are doing and how the pets feel about what's happening. Use a piece of drawing paper for your comic strip. Give your comic strip a name.

Assignment 34 | The Three M's of May

Skills: reference: dictionary; art: drawing; writing: letter

The Three M's of May Background for Teachers

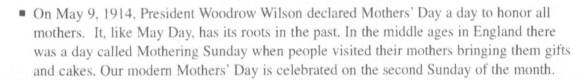

- May Day, Mothers' Day, and Memorial Day: the three M's of May!

- May Day is a very old holiday handed down from the Romans who honored Flora, the goddess of flowers on that day. Children danced around garlanded columns in her temple. The Maypole, a tall pole decorated with ribbons, is our substitute for the garlanded columns in present day celebrations.

- On May 9, 1914, President Woodrow Wilson declared Mothers' Day a day to honor all mothers. It, like May Day, has its roots in the past. In the middle ages in England there was a day called Mothering Sunday when people visited their mothers bringing them gifts and cakes. Our modern Mothers' Day is celebrated on the second Sunday of the month.

- The third M of May, Memorial Day, was first celebrated on May 30, 1868. It was started in the South after the Civil War when people who had lost relatives in the war laid flowers on the graves of soldiers from both the North and South. This observance spread and today the dead are honored on this day throughout the states on the fourth Monday in May.

The Three M's of May Activities

1. What do the students know about the three M's of May? Fill in their gaps with information about the days.

2. Ask if the students have any family traditions about how they celebrate those days? Example: breakfast in bed for Mom or taking flowers to the cemetery on Memorial Day.

3. Review or teach how to write a letter with heading, greeting, and closing.

✔ **Assessment:** Share with the class the reason for Memorial Day, the way we honor the dead, and the reasons for being happy that Spring has come. Partner students to share letters and score letters on neatness.

The Three M's of May Student Handout

Name _____ Date _____

1. There are three special days we celebrate in May. The first day of May is May Day. The second Sunday of the month is Mothers' Day. The last Monday of the month is Memorial Day.

   One of the things we celebrate on May Day is the arrival of spring.

   We honor all mothers on Mothers' Day.

   Use the dictionary to find out who we honor on Memorial Day. What would be some ways to honor them?

   _____

   _____

   _____

2. Imagine a tall pole with bright colored ribbons twined around it. Long ribbons come from the top of the pole down to the ground. Children hold the ends of the long ribbons and dance around the Maypole singing and celebrating that Spring has come. Why do you think there is a celebration for the arrival of Spring? Draw a picture of a maypole here with dancing children and, next to it, make a list of reasons why people are happy spring has come.

3. Mothers' Day is celebrated on the second Sunday in May. On that day we honor our mothers, grandmothers, step-mothers, and any other people who act as our mother.

   Who do you honor on that day? _____

   If you could give that person or those persons anything in the world on that day, what gift would they most like? _____

   You may not be able to buy the gift they would like most, but you can write to them and tell them what you think it would be and why you would like to give it to them. The letter would be a good gift to give and would show how special you think they are.

   On another piece of paper, write a letter to someone you honor on Mothers' Day. Tell them why you think they are special. Tell them about the gift you would like to give them. You might want to draw a picture to go with your letter.

Assignment 35 | Ringling Brothers Circus

Skills: math: addition; art: diorama and drawing; writing: fiction

Ri)ngling Brothers Circus Background for Teachers

- Under the big top – can anyone who's been there ever forget the smells, the sounds, the roar of the crowd? The Ringling brothers, Alf, Al, Charles, John, and Otto and later brothers, Henry, and A.G. Gus, who were known as the "Kings of the Circus World," brought that world to thousands of Americans.

- The Ringling Brothers' tented circus began in May, 1884 and was known as "Ringling Bros. United Monster Shows, Great Double Circus, Royal European Menagerie, Museum, Caravan, and Congress of Trained Animals." Says it all, doesn't it?

- By 1889, tickets were 50 cents for adults, 25 cents for children. Circus tents were big enough for 4,000 people. That year the circus began traveling by train.

- In 1907, The Ringling Brothers bought the other great giant circus, Barnum and Bailey, but didn't merge the two until 1919. When the circuses merged, it took 100 double railroad cars to transport it and its1200 workers.

- Because of financial difficulties, the circus gave its final performance under the Big Top on July 16, 1956. However, thanks to a gentlemen named Irvin Field, the circus was revived and performances are now given in arenas instead of the Big Top.

- The Ringling Brothers' official web site is at http://www.ringling.com.

Ringling Brothers Circus Activities

1. List all the acts you might see at a circus and all the workers that are needed to see that the performers have what they need.

2. Share experiences students have had at a circus.

3. Mini-math lesson: review carrying.

 Assessment: Display dioramas. Go over math and pros and cons of circus life as a class. Share stories and illustrations in small groups. Score story on mechanics.

Ringling Brothers Circus Student Handout

Name _____ Date _____

1. There are many acts in a circus. There are the performers walking on wires stretched high above the crowd; animal trainers leading lions and tigers as they jump through hoops and perform other tricks; clowns in enormous floppy shoes riding on unicycles or in tiny cars; men and women dressed like ballet dancers doing daring tricks on horseback as they race around the circus ring; performers who swallow swords or eat fire; and jugglers, who keep several balls or wooden pins spinning in the air.

   Choose two or three of these acts or other acts you have seen in a circus and make a diorama showing the performers.

2. This is the story of the Ringling Brothers Circus. Fill in the right years.

   A. The Ringling brothers began their circus in 1884. Five years later, in _____ the circus had grown so big it had to use trains to carry the equipment and workers from city to city.

   B. Eight years after that, in _____, the Ringling Brothers Circus bought another big circus, Barnum and Bailey.

   C. Twelve years later, in _____, the circuses joined forces.

   D. In _____, thirty-seven years after the two circuses joined, the Ringling Brothers gave their last performance in a tent. Arenas are now the place where circus acts perform.

3. Circus people are always going from place to place. They usually do not have a home where they live all year round. This can be good in some ways and not so good in others. Make two lists.

   Put a happy face on the top of one list for all the good things about traveling so much.

   Put a sad face on top of the list of things you think would not be so good about traveling so much.

4. If you were going to be a circus performer, which act would you like to perform? What kind of costume would you wear? What would you do in your act? What would you like best about being part of the circus? On another piece of paper, draw who you would want to be. Imagine you are that person and write a story about your life in the circus.

Assignment 36 | Beetles and Bugs

Skills: science: invertebrates; reference: encyclopedia; writing: fiction

Beetles and Bugs Background for Teachers

- Invertebrates are animals with no backbone. Insects are small invertebrates with bodies divided into three segments: a head, a thorax, and an abdomen. They belong to the category of invertebrates called arthropods. Usually adult insects will have three pairs of legs, one pair of antennae, two bulging eyes called compound eyes because they are divided into many six-sided compartments, and they may have one or two pair of wings or no wings at all. They also have a hard exoskeleton. Insects live in almost every habitat on earth.

- Some common insects are mosquitoes, ants, honey bees, moths, flies, grasshoppers, moths, butterflies, beetles, crickets, roaches, and fleas.

- The group of invertebrates called arachnids includes spiders, ticks, mites, and scorpions. They are not insects because they have eight legs and only two main body segments, the cephalothorax and the abdomen.

- Insects are both helpful and harmful to man. They can bite and sting, they spread diseases, and they sometimes ruin a farmer's crops. On the other hand, they eat wastes as well as dead animals and plants, and they pollinate plants which enables crops to grow.

Beetles and Bugs Activities

1. Place several books about invertebrates in the classroom and encourage students to share what they know or have read about them.

2. Draw or show and post pictures of an arthropod and an arachnid.

3. Review the classes of invertebrates you are studying: arthropods and arachnids.

4. Review how to keep a tally: four upright lines with the fifth crossing.

 Assessment: Chart the invertebrates the students have found and discuss difference in numbers and if season would make a difference. Group students to share stories. Score written assignment on creativity. Post pictures of invertebrates.

Beetles and Bugs Student Handout

Name _____ Date _____

1. Some of the smallest animals in the world are called invertebrates. These animals do not have a backbone like you do. The two kinds of invertebrates that we see around our homes and neighborhoods are insects and spiders.

   Insects: roaches, mosquitoes, ants, bees, grasshoppers, moths, flies, beetles, crickets, fleas, and butterflies. These are called **arthropods.** They have three main body parts, the head, thorax, and abdomen, and six legs.

   Spiders, mites, and ticks are called **arachnids**. They have two main body parts, the cephalothorax and abdomen, and eight legs.

   Look in the encyclopedia for a picture of insects and spiders. On the back of this paper, draw an example of each one. Label the pictures "Arthropod" (insects) and "Arachnid" (spiders). Label the head, thorax, and abdomen of the arthropod and the cephalothorax and abdomen of the arachnid.

2. For a few days, watch out for arthropods and arachnids around your house, in your neighborhood, anywhere you go. Keep a tally below.

   Arthropods (insects)   Arachnids (spiders)

   What beetles or bugs did you see the most of? _____

   _____

   Were they arthropods (insects) or arachnids (spiders)? _____

   Do you think the numbers would be different in a different season of the year? If yes, when? _____

   _____

3. Scary stories are sometimes about insects or spiders that have grown huge and terrorized people. Choose one of the beetles or bugs we have been studying and, on another piece of paper, write a story that tells how it grew so large, what it did to scare people, and how it was captured. Draw a picture to go with your story.

Chapter 10 | June

JUNE						
				1	2	3
4	5	6	7	8	9	10
11	12	13	14	15	16	17
18	19	20	21	22	23	24
25	26	27	28	29	30	

Assignment 37 | Rivers of the World

Skills: geography: continents, rivers, maps; critical thinking; reference: encyclopedia; math: subtraction; writing: essay

Rivers of the World Background for Teachers

- A river is a body of freshwater, fed by springs and streams, that flows down to a lake or sea. The channel is where the river flows. The floodplain is the flat area on either side of the channel.

- A river begins on hillsides as small rills or channels. Several small rills join to make larger and larger channels until a river is formed. Rivers carry silt and water to the sea.

- Here are some of the major rivers of the world.

   Africa: Nile, 4160 miles, the longest river in the world
   Asia: Yangtze River in China, 3900 miles
   Australia: Murray River with tributary Darling River, 3300 miles
   Europe: Volga, 2300 miles
   North America: Missouri, 2540 miles
   South America: Amazon, 4000 miles

- Because Antarctica's surface is a sheet of ice, in fact almost all the earth's ice lies there, it is the only continent not included in the above list.

Rivers of the World Activities

1. Review the names of the seven continents and find them on a world map.

2. On a world map, find the major rivers listed above and note what body of water they each empty into.

3. Discuss the benefits of living near a river: seaports are important for travel and import/export of goods, soil near rivers is rich, fish live in rivers, and a river's wetlands provide a home for migratory birds.

 Assessment: Share local and other river information and math answers. Group the students to share the essays and score them on content. If time permits, make a classroom chart showing the pros and cons of living by a river.

Rivers of the World Student Handout

Name _____ Date _____

1. A river is a body of fresh water that carries water and sediment (dirt, rocks) to the sea. Look at a map of your state. What is the closest river to your home? What body of water does it empty into?

   _____

   _____

2. Next to each of the six continents listed here, write the name of one of its rivers.

Continent	River
Africa	
Asia	
Australia	
Europe	
North America	
South America	

3. Here are some of the longest rivers of the world.

   Nile, 4160 miles
   Yangtze River, 3900 miles
   Volga, 2300 miles
   Missouri, 2540 miles
   Amazon, 4000 miles

   What river is the longest? _____

   What is the second longest? _____

   What is the difference in miles between them? _____

   What is the shortest river in the list? _____

   What is the difference in miles between it and the Nile River? _____

4. Why would it be good to live by a river? Why would it not be so good to live by a river? On another piece of paper, write at least two paragraphs telling why you would like to live by a river and why you would not like to live by a river.

Assignment 38 | The Statue of Liberty

Skills: critical thinking; art: drawing; geography: oceans; writing: essay

The Statue of Liberty Background for Teachers

- The French and the United States have been friends since France helped the Americans in their fight for independence from England. To commemorate that friendship, France gave the Statue of Liberty to the United States. After being exhibited in France, the statue arrived in the United States on June 19, 1885. President Grover Cleveland formally dedicated the statue on October 28, 1886.

- Although most people refer to the statue as the Statue of Liberty, her real name is "Liberty Enlightening the World." The chains of tyranny lie at her feet. In her right hand she holds a torch symbolizing liberty while in her left hand she holds a tablet with the date, July 4, 1776, written in Roman numerals. The seven rays of her crown represent seven seas and the seven continents. French sculptor Frederic Auguste Bartholde designed the statue, and contributions from the French people paid for it. Joseph Pulitzer raised money to pay for the pedestal.

- In 1903, a poem written by American poet Emma Lazurus was inscribed in bronze at the base of the statue. The most famous lines from "The New Colossus" are "Give me your tired, your poor, your huddled masses yearning to breathe free."

The Statue of Liberty Activities

1. Locate France on a world map and discuss its location compared to the location of the United States. Name the ocean that separates them.

2. Discuss how France helped the US during the Revolutionary War and how the US helped France during both World Wars.

3. Talk about any statues the students have seen and how a sculptor does his work.

 Assessment: Share theories about what a torch symbolizes, and share pictures of sculptures, the freedoms they enjoy, and how their picture illustrates the freedoms. Divide class into groups to read their essays. Score the essay on mechanics.

The Statue of Liberty Student Handout

Name _____ Date _____

1. The Statue of Liberty is often the first thing people see when they come to the United States. In one hand the statue holds a torch with a burning flame. Why do you think the person, the sculptor, who made the statue used a torch to welcome people?

   _____

   _____

2. French sculptor Frederic Auguste Bartholde designed "Liberty Enlightening the World" commonly called the Statue of Liberty. Sculptors start with an idea and usually sketch their idea on paper. Then they slowly carve a piece of stone until they have the figure they want.

   Now, pretend you are a sculptor. You need to carve a statue that will show what freedom means to the people of your country. On the back of this paper, sketch a picture of something that represents freedom. Under your sketch, explain what freedoms you enjoy as a citizen of your country and why your figure is a symbol for freedom.

3. The Statue of Liberty was a gift to the United States from France. Look on a map or globe and find France. What ocean does it border? _____

   Look at the east coast of the United States. What ocean is there? _____

   If you take a close look at a map or globe you will see that all the oceans are connected, but they have different names in different parts of the world. Make a list here of all the names given to oceans.

   _____   _____

   _____   _____

   _____   _____

   _____

4. France gave the Statue of Liberty to the United States to show that it was a friend. The people of the United States were very happy to receive the beautiful statue. They put it in New York Harbor so people coming from all over the world can see it.

   What is the best gift you ever received? Did you get it on a birthday or on a holiday that your family celebrates? Was it a surprise or did you know it was coming? On another piece of paper tell about your best gift ever and why you liked it so much.

Assignment 39 | Looking Back

Skills: critical thinking; health: self knowledge; oral presentation

 ## Looking Back Background for Teachers

- Even though subject matter and study skills are routinely reviewed throughout the school year, looking back over the entire year helps to summarize growth and learning over 10 months. It also gives students a chance to see what they did well, how they could have done better, and points them in a direction for what they should aim for in their next year of study.

- In addition to the activities and the handout included in this assignment, ask the students what else they can do to review the past year and make plans for the next. How could they organize their review? How can they map out plans for the next year? Would graphic organizers like charts or graphs help? Would it be helpful to have input from their peers or family?

- Looking back over the year can also be of benefit to the teacher. What lessons went particularly well? How could you have improved others? What did you include this year that was superfluous? What didn't you include in this year's curriculum that should be added next year?

Looking Back Activities

1. With the students, list all the subjects studied this year in class.

2. Construct a bar graph showing the most favorite and the least liked subjects.

3. Discuss why these two subjects were chosen. This information could be very helpful to you when planning for next year.

✓ **Assessment:** Divide the class into small groups to share answers to questions one and two. Post chart paper around the room with one subject at the top of each paper. As students share what they learned in those subjects, write it on the appropriate paper. When you are done you will have a record of all you have covered this year. Have the students make their presentations to the whole class and discuss the ideas for getting along with others and making friends. Score presentation on body language.

Looking Back Student Handout

Name _____ Date _____

1. A) What is the school subject you like best? _____

   Why? _____

   _____

   B) What is the one you like least? _____

   Why? _____

   _____

2. A) What subject did you do the best in this year? _____

   Why do you think you did so well in that subject? _____

   _____

   _____

   B) What subject do you want to improve in next year? _____

   How will you do that? _____

   _____

   _____

   _____

3. Choose a school subject. On the back of this paper, list everything you learned in that subject this year.

   Example: **Math**

   Adding columns

   Adding money

   Adding very big numbers

   Adding fractions....................

4. Going to school is not just about schoolwork. It is also about making friends and getting along with others. Think about this past year. Is there anything you would do differently to get along with others and make friends? On another piece of paper write a few paragraphs about the best ways to do those things. What will you do in exactly the same way? What will you do differently? Practice saying out loud what you have written so you can share your ideas with your classmates.

Assignment 40 | A Dream Vacation

*Skills: health: self knowledge; reference: encyclopedia; graphic organizer;
chart; art: drawing; writing: postcard*

A Dream Vacation Background for Teachers

- June is a common month for planning and taking vacations.
  People plan their trips according to their tastes. To some people,
  relaxing at home, having time to read, or engaging in favorite hobbies while following no set
  schedule is the perfect vacation. To others, a vacation isn't a vacation unless they're visiting
  a far away place, sightseeing, shopping, and meeting new people. Then there are always
  those who are happy either way; staying at home or traveling can be pleasurable to them.

- Learning about what vacations your students prefer can tell you a lot about their
  personalities as well as give them some insight about themselves.

- Sometimes, in the mercenary society in which we live, students get the idea that you
  have to spend a lot of money to enjoy yourself, whether on vacation or not. This is a
  good time to explore what is available in your community so the students can take
  advantage of the activities during their vacation time. Libraries often have free programs;
  zoos are fairly inexpensive; many museums have activity rooms for hands-on experiences
  and fun; bus or tram rides through the city can be an adventure.

A Dream Vacation Activities

1. Discuss previous vacations you and the students have taken. Find places on a map.

2. Ask the students to talk about their favorite things to do while on vacation.

3. Discuss their families. Does everyone in the family like the same food, the same kind of
   clothes, the same music, the same kind of vacation? Is it okay to have different tastes?

4. Distribute pieces of sturdy paper cut in the shape and size of a postcard.

 Assessment: Share feelings about vacations. Compare charts and make a master list of local
activities to post in the classroom. You could make copies of the list to send home with
students. Partner students to share postcards and book lists. Score the postcard on mechanics.

A Dream Vacation Handout

Name _____ Date _____

1. Everybody likes to take a vacation. Some people like to travel away from their homes for a vacation. Others enjoy staying at home and relaxing.

   What do you like to do -- stay at home or go to another place?

   _____

   Why do you like that kind of a vacation?

   _____

   _____

   _____

2. Imagine two different vacations.

   Vacation One: You are given enough money to go visit anywhere in the world for a vacation. Where would you go?

   Vacation Two: You must spend your vacation staying near your home.

   Now make a chart on the back of this paper. On one side of the chart write Vacation One and the name of the place you would visit. Read about the place you picked and make a list of what you could do there.

   On the other side of the chart, write Vacation Two and the name of your hometown or city. Under it research and list all the things there are for you to do near your home.

3. When you are on vacation you will have time to read. Look in the library and find the names of three books you would like to read on your vacation. Write the titles of the books and the authors here.

Title of Book	Author

4. Paste or draw a picture of a place where you would like to go on vacation on one side of the "postcard" your teacher has given you. Divide the other side into two parts. In the left hand part, write a note to a friend telling him or her what you are doing and if you are having a good time. In the right hand part, write your friend's name and address.

Reference

Dictionary

Encyclopedia

Science

Writing

Autobiography

Biography

Description

Directions

Essay

Fiction

Interview

Letters

Poetry

Reviews

Sequencing

Slogans